Cindy Beckman

**Library of Congress
Cataloging-in-Publication Data**

Vail, Linda.
  Dining on deck.

  Includes index.
  1. Cookery, Marine. I. Title.
TX840.M7V35 1986   614.5'753   86-9160
ISBN 0-913589-25-X
ISBN 0-913589-21-7 (pbk.)

Cover photograph: Jim Raycroft,
                  Raycroft/McCormick, Boston
Cover design: Trezzo-Braren Studio
Typography: Villanti & Sons, Printers, Inc.
Printing: Capital City Press

Williamson Publishing Co.
Box 185
Charlotte, Vermont 05445
(800) 234-8791

Manufactured in the United States of America

10

Notice: The information contained in this book is
true, complete and accurate to the best of our
knowledge. All recommendations and suggestions
are made without any guarantees on the part of
the author or Williamson Publishing. The author
and publisher disclaim all liability incurred in con-
nection with the use of this information.

DINING ON DECK

FINE FOODS FOR SAILING & BOATING

LINDA VAIL

design and illustrations by Loretta Trezzo

WILLIAMSON PUBLISHING
CHARLOTTE, VERMONT 05445

CONTENTS

For Burr

FOREWORD

$\mathscr{S}$ix years ago my husband and I bought our first sailboat. We are now on sailboat number three—a thirty-three-foot sloop, fully equipped for cruising. I can think of nothing more pleasant on a beautiful summer's day than setting out for the day, an overnight, a weekend, or a more extended period of time on the boat. It is, for me, the most relaxing way to savor those special summer hours.

In keeping with that, our whole lifestyle becomes more relaxed, more casual. However, casual does not mean eating hot dogs and beans, nor opening up a "can of something" for dinner. Dining on the boat is an occasion greeted with much anticipation. Dining—not simply eating—has become the rule of cruising. Our appetites seem heightened, perhaps as a result of being in the fresh air, but also because we make dining the focal point of the day. We feel pleasantly indulged as we bask in the ambiance of the water, the sky, the good food, and good company. There is no question that food is an important element in a sailor's life. The key is incorporating that element in a way that is in keeping with relaxing and having a wonderful time.

I enjoy entertaining friends and family. It is important to me that each occasion be somehow special and impart a quiet kind of elegance. That doesn't mean using my finest china and linens, nor creating epicurean masterpieces with a high degree of difficulty. For me it simply means creating an illusion of ease and grace that makes everyone feel pampered. My greatest pleasure comes from orchestrating each event.

It is at the prompting of my wonderful husband and my dear friends, particularly Beth, that I set about the task of organizing my thoughts and my favorite recipes to share some of my experience with you. I love to cook and to entertain; unfortunately, as a working wife and mother, I don't have as much time as I would like to do either. I have to be efficient. I don't have the luxury of spending hours planning or shopping, and if I forget something I usually have to go with an impromptu "Plan B." So, even if you don't particularly enjoy cooking, or your time is at a premium, don't dismiss this book as something that's not meant for you. You are my greatest challenge. I am confident that together we can make the organizing and cooking tasks simpler and more pleasant.

Chapter

1

A Little Planning Goes A Long Way

*G*enerally, I approach cooking with a less is more philosophy. Subtle flavors, an unexpected twist in ingredients, a contrast in a meal's components—it is this under-
stated approach in cooking and in presentation which can
change a meal from simply eating to dining.

When dining onboard, with a backdrop of nature's
beautiful setting, this understatement becomes even more
important. You'll find that a slight move away from the
ordinary can result in the remarkable, and sometimes, in
the extraordinary. A simple chicken sandwich—ordinary;
but when the chicken has been poached in wine and is
sliced extra thin, when the bread is oatmeal, when you use
tarragon mayonnaise instead of plain, and layer on watercress instead of lettuce—well, now you have stepped into
another world. You have the start of a special lunch for a
day sail. Time involved? No more than if you made a run-of-
the-mill sandwich.

This is very much what *Dining On Deck* is about: taking your usual time-frame, your usual preparations, your usual ingredients, your usual energy level and—using those same elements—catapulting your onboard fare to something very special. This book is about organization— of time, of supplies, of energy, even of your galley kitchen. This book is about sharing—the responsibilities, the effort, and the rewards.

Strangely enough, this book is not really about cooking. With few exceptions, I have not drawn on my repertoire of complex recipes. Those recipes and those cuisines have a special place in my life, but not onboard. Instead, I offer to you recipes that are startling in their simplicity, offering ease in preparation, transporting, and final assembly.

The complete menus can be followed as is, mixed and matched, or used simply as a point of inspiration. However, the juxtaposition of a meal's components is important; it is this balance that I have worked to develop. It is a balance not only of foods—their textures, flavors, and appearance—but also a balance in effort. Menus were planned so that a limited amount of onboard preparation, a limited amount of preboarding preparation, and a set amount of prepared foods were all incorporated into each meal and each weekend's plan. You should never feel a slave to your menu; dining on deck is for everyone to enjoy—including the cook.

With this in mind, I have coded every recipe as to degree of difficulty and relative preparation time involved. All recipes are for 4 servings, unless otherwise noted. The ★ on the menus denotes recipes included in this book.

very easy; little preparation time; often can be done onboard.

moderate; some preparation time involved, most of which can be done preboarding if you choose.

more difficult; advance preparation definitely required.

may be prepared well in advance and frozen.

USE HIGH QUALITY INGREDIENTS

Even though this is not a gourmet cookbook as such, these recipes combine to form sophisticated menus. Everything you do will improve upon the final product. Thus, always use the best quality ingredients available to you, and still allow yourself to pinch hit when necessary. Fresh is best but onboard it's not always practical. If you have access to fresh herbs (and I urge you to grow some anywhere possible in the summer), then use them (1 tablespoon fresh is about 1 teaspoon dried). Likewise for fruits, vegetables, fish—if fresh is available, then buy it, but keep in mind you can still work wonders with canned crabmeat or frozen whole green beans. For chicken broth, homemade is again best, but in the summer who is going to prepare it? Select the best brand available to you—there is a difference! And when it comes to mayonnaise, do take the time to make a really good blender or food processor mayonnaise; it makes a world of difference on a sandwich or in a salad. Try my basic recipe on page 53, and then try lots of variations for subtly flavored mayonnaises.

KEEPING FOODS FRESH

Cooked rice, pasta and potatoes do not keep well in an icebox. If these are to be salad ingredients, it is best to make the salad ahead of time. It will keep very well. If that's not possible, take the raw ingredients and prepare your salad from scratch onboard.

Give yourself as much ice surface as possible, and be sure to keep things that spoil quickly, such as meat and fish, in direct contact with the ice.

Keep fresh vegetables away from direct contact with the ice, since they will freeze and wilt.

Breads and pastries stay fresher in the icebox; they do not need to be in direct contact with the ice.

It helps to be organized at mealtimes for many reasons. Remember that the less time the cover is off the icebox, the longer the cooling effect will be retained.

A WEEKEND SAIL

If you are planning a weekend sail, select a weekend menu. Go through it and make any alterations you wish. Review the recipes (recipes included in this book are marked with an asterisk); make a shopping list (you'll find most ingredients are usual household staples), and jot down the few advance preparations you need to make. Depending on my schedule, I usually shop Thursday on my way home from work, and spend no more than an hour to an hour and a half in preparation Friday before boarding.

Here is how I might plan my schedule in preparation for Weekend Sail Menu I (see page 58).

Wednesday

20–60 minutes

First, I review the menu for the weekend and come up with a general list of ingredients. I check my cupboards to see what I already have on hand, and give some thought to what I have stocked on the boat. Then I prepare my shopping list. If I have the ingredients and the energy, I'll bake the Amaretto Cheesecake Cookies on Wednesday evening. I also take a minute to call our guests and give out meal assignments. Usually, I have guests assume responsibility for breakfasts or one breakfast and one lunch. That takes me off the hook for nearly everything but dinner, which I enjoy preparing. I often ask guests to prepare something specific unless they have a dish they particularly want to cook. It's good to check this out—especially with non-sailors—or you'll end up with a great idea best left on shore. Generally, people love to pitch in and will be receptive to a simple yet elegant suggestion.

Thursday

60 minutes (not including shopping)

I grocery shop on my way home from work. This is when I usually begin to seriously organize both in my mind and in actual packing up. I organize the food—dry food and canned goods get packed in bags or crates ready to pick up and transport. Don't bother to unload your groceries into your cupboards, and then pack up the next day. Save yourself the steps and unload right into your carrying crates. I'll mix up the roll dough for Friday's dinner and let it rise overnight in the refrigerator, and I marinate the meat for Saturday night. I may also bake the Chocolate Cake for Saturday night if I've got the time and energy. (If I'm pressed for time, I may buy all the baked goods for the weekend, since I've scouted out the best bake shops in my locale.) Be flexible! Lastly, I check to make sure dishpans were refilled with water and put in the freezer after the last outing; if not we fill the dishpans and get them in the freezer.

Friday

90 minutes

I bake the rolls while someone else cooks Saturday morning's bacon and washes the weekend's vegetables. Then we organize the fresh food, ice, and beverages. I usually invite my guests for the 90 minutes of preparations before boarding. We all pitch in with the last minute chores, which makes them go quickly and we have fun working together. If you are one who prefers silence for final organization and preparation, then at least have your guests arrive early enough to help you pack up everything.

SIMPLIFY ONBOARD LIFE

PACKAGING

I tend to repackage things into appropriate amounts for recipes, or in some cases in containers that are sturdier than the store packaging.

I'm careful about packing things in containers that are *just* the right size. Remember it is not enough to have good tasting foods; you want the food to look appealing too. Choose a container that protects the food from movement, from layering, from moisture build-up. When I prepare deviled eggs, for example, I use a shallow square or rectangular container with a tight fitting lid, the exact size to accommodate the eggs. Line the bottom with a layer of absorbent paper towels. This both prevents the eggs from sliding around and absorbs excess moisture. As long as the eggs don't get turned upside down, it works beautifully. I tend to pack foods such as brownies with equal care. Again, a square or rectangular container lined this time with waxed paper. Use waxed paper between layers, too, as brownies tend to stick together and once they do, their aesthetic appeal is gone.

There are all types, shapes and sizes of food containers available. There are many with very specific uses, such as pie and cake containers, coffee cans, celery, butter, and on and on. Obviously, there are many brands. My personal favorites tend to be Tupperware and Rubbermaid for both their quality and variety of sizes and uses.

TRANSPORTING

Transporting provisions out to the boat can be another challenge unless you have the proper equipment. Take care here to handle your foods gently, as this is the one place carelessness takes its toll. Pack food systematically and sensibly (right side up, crushables on top). There are wonderful canvas bags in a variety of sizes available from most sporting goods stores and catalogues. There are also collapsible crates, much like milk crates, but much better because once you have them on board, they fold up for convenient storage. It's worth arranging for generous packing space and then stowing away your crates, rather than trying to juggle or balance too many items in too few carrying crates.

GARBAGE

Unpleasant though it may be, I have found some ways of creating less garbage and therefore lessening the problem. First, and perhaps most obvious, is the elimination of bones wherever possible; use boneless pork chops, boneless steaks, boneless chicken breasts. You may pay a bit of a premium for these, but it's well worth it in the end. I also make every effort to prepare exact amounts of recipes so there are few leftovers and what there are can be re-used in a salad, cold plate, or sandwich. If it is just the two of us sailing, I often don't make special plans for lunches for that reason—just about anything leftover can be turned into a pleasing salad. Though the temptation may be strong to use paper plates and cups, don't. The garbage collects too rapidly and it is so much nicer to use dishes.

BEVERAGES

It pays to buy beer and soda in cans. They don't break and they are much lighter than bottles are, especially when empty. We are big fans of seltzer both for cocktails and as a refreshing drink with lime. I have found having a seltzer bottle aboard saves much carting of bottles or cans. We keep our beverages in a cooler in our sail locker. We find we don't have to go below just to get a cold drink, plus it saves on the ice in the icebox which doesn't get opened as much.

ICE & PERISHABLES

Keeping plenty of ice in the icebox is crucial to the success of food storage. If you don't have refrigeration on your boat, you can freeze large blocks of ice in rectangular dishpans. It lasts much longer than the smaller purchased blocks. We generally prepare two large blocks for a weekend sail, and then I use the dishpans for washing and rinsing dishes while onboard. It is very important to keep an eye on your ice situation.

Two things you can do to preserve your ice are limit the number of times you open the icebox and keep it filled to capacity. Using a separate cooler for beverages is one way to limit opening the icebox, but also organizing your food can help you avoid keeping it open while you search through Sunday's breakfast ingredients in order to prepare Friday's dinner.

Also, remember that freezing foods (meats, cooked vegetables, breads, pastries, milk, cream, fruit juices) not only prolongs their freshness, but also adds to the cooling capacity and extended life of your ice.

Perishables won't last as long in your icebox as they would in your refrigerator at home, so plan to use your most perishable items within a few days. Freeze anything you can that won't be used within the first couple of days.

VEGETABLES AND FRUITS

I always wash my vegetables and fruits at home. Leafy greens can be patted dry, rolled in paper towels, and stored in plastic bags in the icebox—not touching the ice.

SOUP

I find that on occasions when I have planned a hot soup or stew for lunch and we won't be anchoring until the end of the day, I can heat the soup in the morning, after breakfast, and put it in a thermos. That way I don't have to go down in the galley and cook under sail—something I personally do not especially enjoy.

PREPARED FOODS

There is always a place for prepared foods onboard. Now with specialty shops abounding even in the most out-of-the-way places, you can still dine quite nicely on short notice. Especially if you have an aversion to warm weather baking, supplement your menus with a stop at a fine bakery.

It is always a good idea to keep some canned meals on board. Canned ham, tuna, beef stew, hash, Chinese food, vegetables, soups, spaghetti sauce provide good emergency back-up in case your supplies run out before you anticipated. My philosophy is to use these as the exception rather than the rule, but I, too, derive a measure of security in knowing these supplies are onboard should the need arise.

Chapter

2

ONBOARD:
THE PLANNING PAYS OFF

*S*o now you and your guests are onboard. With surprisingly little extra effort, you can look forward to a wonderful outing and some fine dining, too. I think you'd have to agree with me—dining on deck is as much attitude as effort.

But I want to show you without a shadow of a doubt how your planning pays off, how you can relax, enjoy, soak up the sun, the wind, the exhilaration of the moment as much as your guests. All it takes along with planning and a flexible game plan is a well-organized galley, a well-equipped galley, and some careful provisioning.

ORGANIZING THE GALLEY

Organizing the galley is a critical task when the goal is to create elegant meals with a minimum of effort at the time of preparation. Aboard my own boat—a 33-foot sloop—I have organized the galley in such a way that all the things I typically use in the preparation of a meal are close at hand in a triangular configuration. Following, you can see a floor plan and elevation of the boat interior with particular attention being paid to the galley.

The galley is a very small area, yet, there seems to be ample storage when planned carefully. Above the sink there is only a paper towel dispenser. Below the sink is storage for trash/garbage, trash bags, cleaning supplies and dishwashing supplies. As you face the stove/oven wall, you find the main bulk of the "kitchen" storage. At the wall there is a small shelf where I store herbs and spices, matches, oil candle, toothpicks, clothespins and pot holders. Below the shelf there is a closed storage area where I have ample room for dishes, glasses, and flatware for eight people, plus the coffee pot, cutting board, wraps and plastic bags, covered plastic containers, cooking utensils, salad/mixing bowls, measuring cups, foam can holders and liquor. Behind and below the stove is room for pots, pans and serving trays.

I am very fortunate in that my icebox holds enough provisions for two people for two weeks. The dry storage compartment holds all the staples, plus whatever munchies, crackers, and cookies I choose to take aboard. Below the chart table (opposite the galley wall) there is ample storage for large items such as dishpans, folded carrying crates, or whatever.

I find that the acrylic stemware can be easily stored in the small compartment under the first seat in the dining area. The area behind the bench on the opposite wall (next to the oven) has become storage for soda, wine, seltzer, cordials, canned juices, etc. Next to that is ample storage for linens, both kitchen and bath.

There are lots of ways to organize storage on a boat and every boat is designed differently. It is important to plan the storage carefully so you are not dealing with Fibber McGee's closet every time you go to get something.

Be inventive. Things that typically get stored in a horizontal position at home may get stored vertically on the boat, or vice versa. Keep an open mind and look at the situation as a challenge rather than a problem. And, look to friends. They may be wonderful resources for helpful hints and problem solving ideas.

Personally, I find the whole scale of things a refreshing change of pace from a large house—it just doesn't take nearly the work, and it becomes almost playlike in the need to be organized and at times, ingenious.

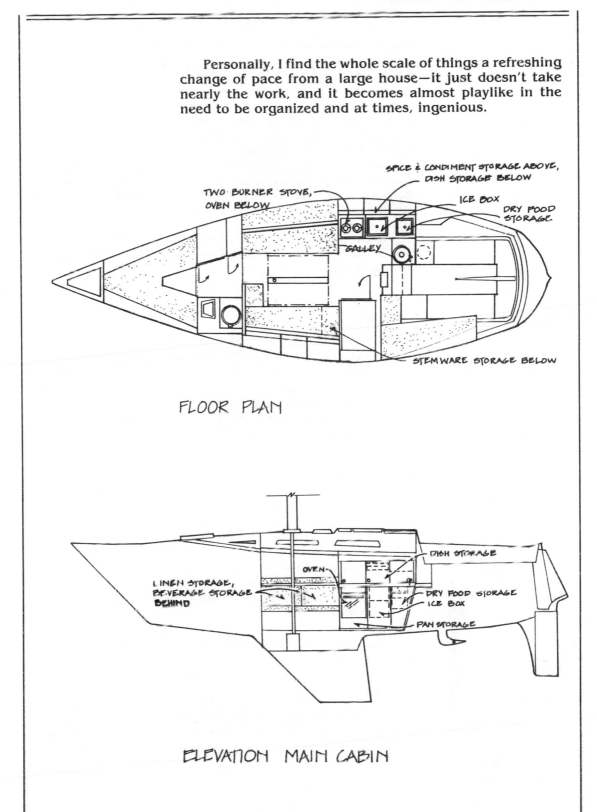

FLOOR PLAN

ELEVATION MAIN CABIN

THE WELL-EQUIPPED GALLEY

It's important to the success of dining well without a lot of work to have the proper equipment on hand. Here, too, you'll find the need for balance and a sense of scale. Obviously you want as many conveniences as are practical for your small space. If you have planned well and done the more complex preparations at home (or saved complex recipes for another time and place), you'll find that you can make a balanced trade-off between equipment and ease.

Following is a list of equipment and accessories that help to make my life onboard easier, without cluttering our limited space.

ESSENTIALS

Set of dishes for 4–8 that stack compactly
There is specialized marine dishware available from a ship's store or marine catalogue. All the pieces have a rubberized ring on the bottom to prevent them from sliding across the table when the boat heals or rough weather is encountered. Worth investigating!

Flatware for 4–8
Here is an area where there are clearly many options. Stainless is the most practical, and a knife with a serrated blade is, in my opinion, the most sensible choice, as it eliminates the need for steak knives. Some of the new flatware with brightly colored handles provides a casual alternative to the more formal patterns we typically use, and is available nearly everywhere from kitchen shops to L.L. Bean.

Barbecue grill with cover (the cover is essential, particularly if you have no oven).

Dishpans
Rubbermaid's heavy duty dishpans are excellent for the purpose of freezing blocks of ice. They are large, easy to handle and they last for years.

Pots and pans (2 covered saucepans, 1½ quart and 2½ quart; 2 10-inch fry pans, one with a cover; 5-quart Dutch oven; small sauté pan). Silverstone-lined steel pans provide easy clean-up and are light-weight—the perfect combination for sailors and boaters. They are available at department and discount stores throughout the country.

Toaster
> The best toaster I have found is a rectangular unit that sets over a burner and toasts two slices of bread lying flat. It can be purchased from Goldberg's Marine Catalogue.

Glasses for beer, soda, etc.; acrylic or plastic

Juice glasses, plastic

Carving set	Paring knife
Wire whisk	Utility knife
Rubber spatula	Measuring cups and spoons
Metal or plastic spatula	Pot holders/oven mitts
Tongs	Ice pick
Large spoons, 1 slotted	First aid kit
Corkscrew	Tool kit
Bottle opener	Coffee pot
Can opener	1 or 2 salad/mixing bowls

NICE TO HAVE

Acrylic or stainless wine glasses
They're wonderful to drink from—far more elegant than regular plastic glasses—and are readily available in department stores, kitchen shops and, of course, marine catalogues.

Thermos
I have one with a pump; the coffee stays hot all day and you needn't remove the lid for service (or spills).

Propane barbecue grill
Available at local discount stores or marine stores. Those from the marine store will probably include a bracket which allows you to hang the grill off the boat. They are, however, significantly more costly and the bracket is available separately and could be adapted to some of the less expensive grills. You may, of course, set the barbecue in the cockpit or on the deck.

Covered containers for leftovers

Plastic bottles with screw caps for milk, juice, etc.

Small cooler
We find it much more convenient for ice cubes than the icebox with all the food, etc.

Tea kettle	Foam can holders
Seltzer bottle	Lamp oil candle
Tea infuser	Meat skewers
Oven	

PROVISIONING

Provisioning your boat for each trip can be greatly simplified by stocking up on staples ahead of time and making sure supplies are replenished as stores get low. Generally, I jot down a list of what needs replenishing as we're packing up at the end of a sail. I also take any packages that are almost empty back home with me to use up rather than having a bit of ketchup to finish up plus a new bottle onboard at once. Don't trust your memory and do write yourself a list; otherwise you end up with three bottles at home and none onboard or vice versa.

Some of the things I find useful to keep on hand include:

Cleaning supplies	Crackers
Paper towels	Cookies
Wraps & plastic bags	Canned soups
Herbs and spices	1 or 2 canned meals
Oil	Canned tuna
Vinegar	Terriyaki sauce
Peanut butter	Steak sauce
Coffee/tea	Worcestershire sauce
Soda	Bottled salad dressing
Juices	Dijon-style mustard
Nuts	A small jar of mayonnaise
Wine and liquor (including cordials)	

HERE WE GO!

When everyone and everything is aboard, it's time to store away the food and the gear. Generally two of us get the boat ready to cast off, while the other two get things ship-shape below.

Now begins a weekend of fun and relaxation. I really make an effort to put aside all sense of entertaining, and get fully involved in our outing right from the start. Once we have anchored, it's time for cocktails and dinner preparations. I purposely try to keep Friday dinner preparations to a minimum, as you'll notice on all the weekend menus. While I begin the rice, someone else may chop tomatoes and crumble the cheese.

Presentation of onboard meals is as important as the food. It is part of what separates the dining experience from simply eating. I often serve right from the galley. It saves on serving dishes, yet each plate can be arranged and garnished attractively with a little thought and no additional effort. It's generally little things like balancing colors, using fresh greens under salads and garnishing with parsley, mint, lemon, pimento or whatever seems most appropriate to the dish.

And don't forget fresh flowers. They can be a wonderfully unexpected surprise and add a very special touch. In other words, little niceties—not fussy, just special in that they are unexpected onboard—have a lot to do with dining on deck. Try linen napkins to add to the ambiance as well. Perhaps not for every meal, but they do lend a special elegance to dinner. Small but not insignificant.

At the meal's end comes the inevitable clean-up. I usually put a kettle of water on while we are having coffee and dessert. When we are finished eating and talking, there's boiling water ready for the dishes (for those of us who don't have hot water). The plates and pans get scraped thoroughly—no disposal on our boat. We set up our dishpans with wash water and rinse water. In warm weather, we usually do dishes out in the cockpit and it really doesn't seem like work at all. Typically, the cook doesn't have to join in the clean-up.

Trash and garbage go in plastic bags that can be closed up to eliminate spills and odors. This is where using boneless cuts of meat and careful packaging really pay off.

Now it's time to relax quietly under the stars and drink in the full wonder of the universe around us.

Chapter

3

A DAY SAIL

$\mathcal{P}$utting together food for a day sail, for me, is much like planning a day in the country or any other kind of single day getaway that takes you completely out of the usual work-a-day world and the routine of your daily life. Each outing becomes an adventure and a special occasion. The food may be very simple, but with a little planning—not necessarily a lot of preparation—you can turn each meal into elegant fare. Wine and cheese, fruit in season, and a loaf of French bread can be a wonderful lunch for a getaway; however, it soon proves to be a bit tiresome. I have therefore, provided a range of lunch menus that will make for delightful days—not lots of work—and a variety of choices.

LUNCH ✦ MENUS

★ Marinated Shrimp & Olives ★
★ Vegetarian Rice Salad ★
Sourdough French Bread
Fresh Fruit

★ Chilled Asparagus Soup ★
★ Country Pâté ★
Brie
French Bread/Sweet Butter
★ Apple Walnut Cake ★

★ Ham Tarts ★
Crudite
★ Sourdough Rolls (see page 60) ★
Fresh Fruit

★ Spinach Pasta Salad with Shrimp & Broccoli ★
★ Garlic Toast ★
★ Blueberry Crisp ★

★ Shrimp, Cauliflower & Snow Peas in Crème Fraîche ★
★ Rye Muffins (see page 47) ★
★ Chocolate, White Chocolate Chunk Cookies ★

★ Smoked Duck Breast Salad ★
★ Artichoke Hearts with Feta Cheese ★
★ Herb Rolls ★
Fresh Melon

★ Avocado with Crabmeat & Continental Sauce ★

Fresh Grapes

Black Bread/Butter

★ Coconut Macaroon Cupcakes ★

★ Almond Soup ★

★ Lobster Eclairs ★

★ Shortbread (see page 103) ★

★ Avocado, Jerusalem Artichoke & Papaya Salad ★

★ Potted Shrimp ★

Crusty French Bread

★ Mixed Fruit Bars ★

★ Shrimp Salad ★

Sliced Tomatoes/Cucumber Sticks

Rolls/Butter

★ Milk Chocolate Fudge ★

★ Danish Sandwiches ★

★ German-style Potato Salad ★

Dill Pickles

★ Almond-filled Brownies ★

Corned Beef & Swiss on Rye

★ Cole Slaw ★

Cold Pack Kosher Dills

★ Lemon Squares ★

★ Tortellini Salad ★

★ Smoked Pheasant with Dill Sauce ★

French Bread

Strawberries with Sour Cream & Brown Sugar

★ Chef's Salad with Shallot Vinaigrette ★

★ Rye Muffins ★

★ Apricot Pound Cake ★

★ Chicken & Watercress Sandwiches ★

★ Cucumber Mint Salad ★

★ Date Pinwheels ★

★ Salad Nicoise ★

French Bread

★ Chocolate Chip Brownies ★

★ Roast Beef Pockets ★

★ Potato Salad ★

Kosher Dill Pickles

★ Jam Bars ★

★ Ham & Cheese Roll-ups ★

★ Chilled Zucchini Soup ★

Fresh Fruit

★ Tomatoes Stuffed with Crabmeat Salad ★

★ Marinated Green Beans ★

Garlic Bagel Chips

★ Mincemeat Cookies ★

★ Curried Chicken Salad ★

Fresh Cantaloupe Slices

Rolls/Butter

★ Chocolate Chip Pound Cake ★

LUNCH • RECIPES

MARINATED SHRIMP & OLIVES

1½ pounds jumbo shrimp, cooked, peeled and deveined

½ pound ripe olives, drained

¾ cup fresh lime juice

¾ cup orange juice

⅓ cup water

4 cloves garlic, chopped

2 tablespoons fennel seed

Peel of 1 lime and 1 orange, cut into thin strips

Avocado slices

1. Combine lime juice, orange juice, water, garlic, fennel seed, and lime and orange peel in a medium-sized container with a tightly fitting lid.

2. Add shrimp and olives; stir to blend well. Cover. Chill at least 24 hours.

3. To serve, drain and garnish with avocado slices.

VEGETARIAN RICE SALAD

2 cups cooked rice

1 16-ounce can cut Blue Lake green beans

1 small can chick peas

1 small red onion, finely chopped

1 large tomato, peeled, seeded and chopped

2 tablespoons fresh chives, chopped

1 tablespoon fresh parsley, chopped

Salt and pepper

2 tablespoons vinegar

½ cup good quality olive oil

Tomato wedges (to garnish)

1. Combine all ingredients except tomato wedges together in a large bowl. Chill several hours or overnight.

2. Serve garnished with fresh tomato wedges.

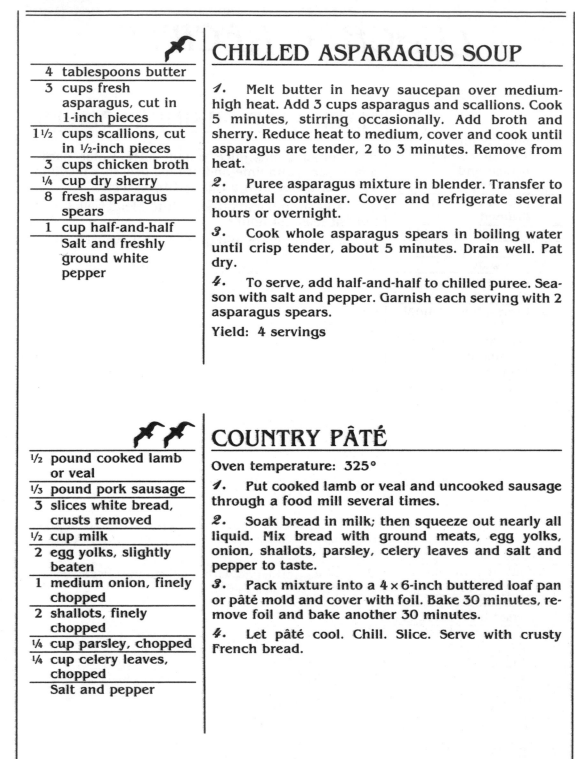

CHILLED ASPARAGUS SOUP

4	tablespoons butter
3	cups fresh asparagus, cut in 1-inch pieces
1½	cups scallions, cut in ½-inch pieces
3	cups chicken broth
¼	cup dry sherry
8	fresh asparagus spears
1	cup half-and-half
	Salt and freshly ground white pepper

1. Melt butter in heavy saucepan over medium-high heat. Add 3 cups asparagus and scallions. Cook 5 minutes, stirring occasionally. Add broth and sherry. Reduce heat to medium, cover and cook until asparagus are tender, 2 to 3 minutes. Remove from heat.

2. Puree asparagus mixture in blender. Transfer to nonmetal container. Cover and refrigerate several hours or overnight.

3. Cook whole asparagus spears in boiling water until crisp tender, about 5 minutes. Drain well. Pat dry.

4. To serve, add half-and-half to chilled puree. Season with salt and pepper. Garnish each serving with 2 asparagus spears.

Yield: 4 servings

COUNTRY PÂTÉ

½	pound cooked lamb or veal
⅓	pound pork sausage
3	slices white bread, crusts removed
½	cup milk
2	egg yolks, slightly beaten
1	medium onion, finely chopped
2	shallots, finely chopped
¼	cup parsley, chopped
¼	cup celery leaves, chopped
	Salt and pepper

Oven temperature: 325°

1. Put cooked lamb or veal and uncooked sausage through a food mill several times.

2. Soak bread in milk; then squeeze out nearly all liquid. Mix bread with ground meats, egg yolks, onion, shallots, parsley, celery leaves and salt and pepper to taste.

3. Pack mixture into a 4 x 6-inch buttered loaf pan or pâté mold and cover with foil. Bake 30 minutes, remove foil and bake another 30 minutes.

4. Let pâté cool. Chill. Slice. Serve with crusty French bread.

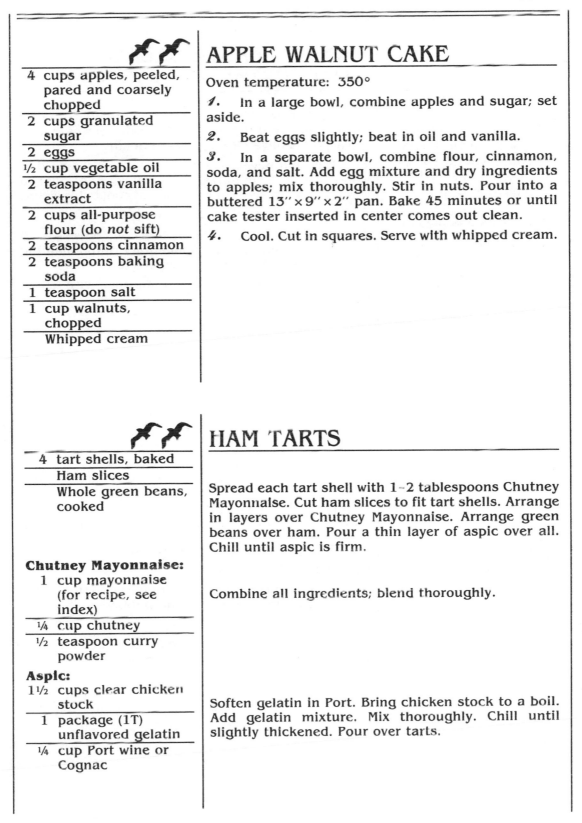

APPLE WALNUT CAKE

4 cups apples, peeled, pared and coarsely chopped
2 cups granulated sugar
2 eggs
½ cup vegetable oil
2 teaspoons vanilla extract
2 cups all-purpose flour (do *not* sift)
2 teaspoons cinnamon
2 teaspoons baking soda
1 teaspoon salt
1 cup walnuts, chopped
   Whipped cream

Oven temperature: 350°

1. In a large bowl, combine apples and sugar; set aside.

2. Beat eggs slightly; beat in oil and vanilla.

3. In a separate bowl, combine flour, cinnamon, soda, and salt. Add egg mixture and dry ingredients to apples; mix thoroughly. Stir in nuts. Pour into a buttered 13" x 9" x 2" pan. Bake 45 minutes or until cake tester inserted in center comes out clean.

4. Cool. Cut in squares. Serve with whipped cream.

HAM TARTS

4 tart shells, baked
   Ham slices
   Whole green beans, cooked

Spread each tart shell with 1-2 tablespoons Chutney Mayonnaise. Cut ham slices to fit tart shells. Arrange in layers over Chutney Mayonnaise. Arrange green beans over ham. Pour a thin layer of aspic over all. Chill until aspic is firm.

Chutney Mayonnaise:
1 cup mayonnaise (for recipe, see index)
¼ cup chutney
½ teaspoon curry powder

Combine all ingredients; blend thoroughly.

Aspic:
1½ cups clear chicken stock
1 package (1T) unflavored gelatin
¼ cup Port wine or Cognac

Soften gelatin in Port. Bring chicken stock to a boil. Add gelatin mixture. Mix thoroughly. Chill until slightly thickened. Pour over tarts.

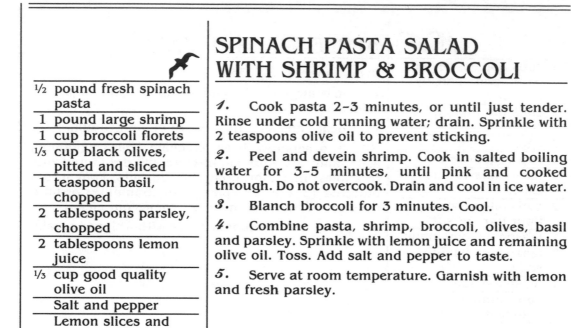

SPINACH PASTA SALAD WITH SHRIMP & BROCCOLI

½ pound fresh spinach pasta

1 pound large shrimp

1 cup broccoli florets

⅓ cup black olives, pitted and sliced

1 teaspoon basil, chopped

2 tablespoons parsley, chopped

2 tablespoons lemon juice

⅓ cup good quality olive oil

Salt and pepper

Lemon slices and fresh parsley (for garnish)

1. Cook pasta 2–3 minutes, or until just tender. Rinse under cold running water; drain. Sprinkle with 2 teaspoons olive oil to prevent sticking.

2. Peel and devein shrimp. Cook in salted boiling water for 3–5 minutes, until pink and cooked through. Do not overcook. Drain and cool in ice water.

3. Blanch broccoli for 3 minutes. Cool.

4. Combine pasta, shrimp, broccoli, olives, basil and parsley. Sprinkle with lemon juice and remaining olive oil. Toss. Add salt and pepper to taste.

5. Serve at room temperature. Garnish with lemon and fresh parsley.

GARLIC TOAST

1 baguette

¼ pound butter

1 head garlic, minced

1. Split baguette in half, lengthwise.

2. Melt butter; add garlic.

3. Brush cut face of bread with garlic butter. Place under broiler until browned and bubbly.

4. Cool. Wrap in foil.

5. At serving time, bread may be reheated, sun-warmed, or served at room temperature.

Topping:
1 cup flour, sifted
¼ cup oats
1 cup light brown sugar, firmly packed
½ cup butter, melted

Filling:
1 pint blueberries
¼ cup brown sugar
2 tablespoons flour
Dash of cinnamon
Crème fraîche for garnish

BLUEBERRY CRISP

Oven temperature: 375°

1. To make topping: In a large bowl combine flour, oats, and brown sugar. Mix well. Stir in melted butter until mixture is crumbly.

2. To make filling: In a lightly greased 8-inch square baking dish, combine blueberries, brown sugar, flour and cinnamon. Stir to mix well.

3. Sprinkle topping evenly over filling. Bake, uncovered, 45 minutes, or until topping is golden and blueberries are cooked. Serve warm or at room temperature with *crème fraîche* (see recipe).

1 pound large shrimp, cooked, peeled and deveined
2 cups cauliflower florets, blanched 5 minutes
1 cup snow peas, blanched 2 minutes
1 teaspoon fresh dill
½ cup *crème fraîche* (see recipe)
Salt and pepper

SHRIMP, CAULIFLOWER & SNOW PEAS IN CRÈME FRAÎCHE

Cool shrimp and vegetables. In a large bowl, combine shrimp, cauliflower, snow peas, and dill. Mix ingredients with *crème fraîche*. Add salt and pepper to taste.

NOTE: This dish is equally delicious served chilled, at room temperature, or hot.

CRÈME FRAÎCHE

½ pint sour cream
1 pint heavy cream

1.   Add sour cream to a saucepan. Blend in heavy cream. Heat gently over low heat until just tepid. (Do not go over 90°.)

2.   Pour mixture into a loosely covered container. Let stand at room temperature for 6–8 hours, or until thickened. Stir, cover tightly, and refrigerate.

CHOCOLATE, WHITE CHOCOLATE CHUNK COOKIES

½ cup unsalted butter, softened
½ cup dark brown sugar, firmly packed
½ cup granulated sugar
1 teaspoon vanilla extract
½ teaspoon salt
⅓ cup cocoa
1 egg
½ teaspoon baking soda
1 cup flour
12 ounces white chocolate, coarsely chopped

Oven temperature: 325°

1.   In a large bowl, combine butter, brown sugar, granulated sugar, vanilla and salt. Beat until fluffy. Beat in cocoa, then egg and baking soda. Stir in flour, then white chocolate chunks. Cover dough and refrigerate at least 1 hour.

2.   Lightly grease baking sheets. Using 2 to 3 tablespoons of dough for each cookie, shape in balls and place on baking sheets 2–3 inches apart. Bake in a preheated oven 12–14 minutes or until cookies spring back when lightly touched. Do not overbake.

3.   Cool on baking sheets for 3 minutes; then transfer to wire racks.

Yield: 18–24 cookies.

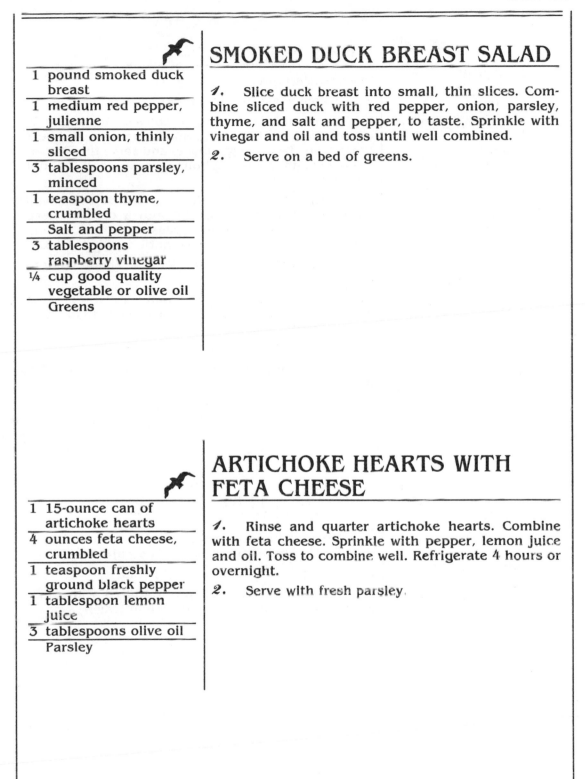

SMOKED DUCK BREAST SALAD

1 pound smoked duck breast

1 medium red pepper, julienne

1 small onion, thinly sliced

3 tablespoons parsley, minced

1 teaspoon thyme, crumbled

Salt and pepper

3 tablespoons raspberry vinegar

¼ cup good quality vegetable or olive oil

Greens

1. Slice duck breast into small, thin slices. Combine sliced duck with red pepper, onion, parsley, thyme, and salt and pepper, to taste. Sprinkle with vinegar and oil and toss until well combined.

2. Serve on a bed of greens.

ARTICHOKE HEARTS WITH FETA CHEESE

1 15-ounce can of artichoke hearts

4 ounces feta cheese, crumbled

1 teaspoon freshly ground black pepper

1 tablespoon lemon juice

3 tablespoons olive oil

Parsley

1. Rinse and quarter artichoke hearts. Combine with feta cheese. Sprinkle with pepper, lemon juice and oil. Toss to combine well. Refrigerate 4 hours or overnight.

2. Serve with fresh parsley.

HERB ROLLS

1	package active dry yeast
¼	cup warm water
¾	cup milk, scalded
3	tablespoons butter
3	tablespoons granulated sugar
1½	teaspoons salt
3–3½	cups all-purpose flour
1	egg, beaten
¼	teaspoon mace
1	tablespoon sage
1	egg white, slightly beaten

Oven temperature: 375°

1. Soften yeast in warm water.

2. Blend milk, butter, sugar, and salt thoroughly in a large bowl; cool to warm. Add 1 cup flour and beat thoroughly. Beat in egg, mace, and sage; then yeast. Mix in enough remaining flour to make a soft (but not sticky) dough.

3. Turn onto a lightly floured surface and knead until smooth and elastic. Put into a greased deep bowl; turn dough to bring greased surface to top. Cover; let rise in a warm place until doubled, 1 hour.

4. Punch down dough and let rest about 10 minutes.

5. Shape dough into 12 round rolls. Place in greased muffin tin cups and let rise again 45 minutes or until doubled.

6. Brush with egg white.

7. Bake in a preheated oven 15 minutes or until browned.

CONTINENTAL SAUCE

6	tablespoons mayonnaise (see recipe)
3	tablespoons sour cream
2	teaspoons Dijon-style mustard
2	teaspoons sherry
3	teaspoons brandy
½	teaspoon paprika
	Parsley and lemon to garnish

1. Mix together mayonnaise, sour cream and mustard. Stir in sherry and brandy. Add paprika.

2. Refrigerate 1 hour before serving.

3. Serve over avocado halves stuffed with crabmeat. Garnish with fresh parsley and lemon.

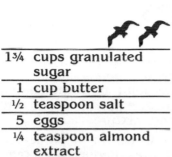

COCONUT MACAROON CUPCAKES

1¾	cups granulated sugar
1	cup butter
½	teaspoon salt
5	eggs
¼	teaspoon almond extract
2	cups all-purpose flour
3	ounces flaked coconut, toasted

Oven temperature: 350°

1. In a large mixer bowl, cream together sugar, butter, and salt until light. Add eggs, one at a time, beating well after each addition. Add almond extract. Fold in flour. Stir in coconut.

2. Line muffin tins with 24 paper baking cups. Fill cups ⅔ full with batter.

3. Bake in a preheated oven for 20–25 minutes or until done. Cool on wire rack.

Yield: 24.

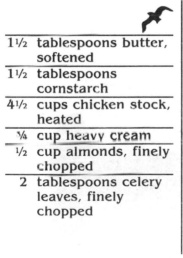

ALMOND SOUP

1½	tablespoons butter, softened
1½	tablespoons cornstarch
4½	cups chicken stock, heated
¼	cup heavy cream
½	cup almonds, finely chopped
2	tablespoons celery leaves, finely chopped

1. In a large saucepan, work cornstarch together with butter. Gradually stir in chicken stock and cook, stirring constantly, for about 5 minutes. Add cream and almonds. Let stand for 30 minutes.

2. Reheat. Pour into thermal container.

3. Serve hot, garnished with chopped celery leaves.

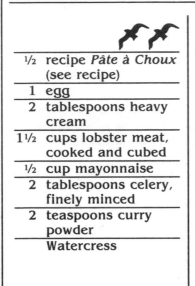

LOBSTER ECLAIRS

½ recipe *Pâte à Choux* (see recipe)

1 egg

2 tablespoons heavy cream

1½ cups lobster meat, cooked and cubed

½ cup mayonnaise

2 tablespoons celery, finely minced

2 teaspoons curry powder

Watercress

Oven temperature: 400°

1. Butter a large baking sheet. Fill a pastry bag fitted with a ⅓-inch plain tube with *pâte à choux*. Pipe out about 16 strips, 3 inches long, onto the baking sheet, about 1 inch apart. Beat egg with cream and brush tops of eclairs with egg mixture.

2. Place the baking sheet in center of preheated oven. Bake eclairs for 10 minutes. Reduce oven temperature to 375° and bake for 10 minutes more. Reduce heat to 350° and continue baking for another 10 minutes. Turn off oven. With the tip of a sharp knife make 1 or 2 slits in each eclair and let the eclairs stand in the oven for 10 to 15 minutes, or until they are dry. Transfer eclairs to a rack and let cool.

3. Put lobster meat in a bowl and fold in mayonnaise. Add celery and curry powder.

4. At serving time, split the eclairs in half lengthwise and divide the lobster mixture among the bottom halves. Place watercress over the filling and replace the tops pressing them down slightly. Garnish with lemon wedges.

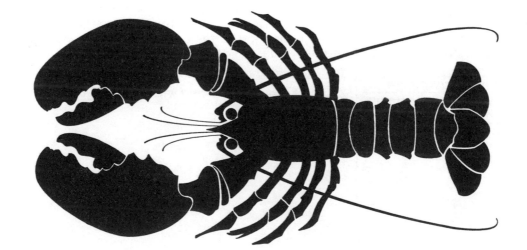

PÂTE À CHOUX

1 cup water
½ cup butter, cut into pieces
¼ teaspoon salt
1 cup flour
3 eggs

1. In a heavy saucepan bring water, butter and salt to a boil over high heat. Lower heat and add flour all at once. With a wooden spoon, beat the mixture until it leaves the sides of the pan and forms a ball.

2. Transfer the dough to the bowl of an electric mixer. With the mixer at high speed, beat in eggs, one at a time, beating thoroughly after each addition. The batter should be just thick enough to hold peaks. If it is too thick, add another egg to bring batter to the right consistency.

AVOCADO, JERUSALEM ARTICHOKE & PAPAYA SALAD

2 avocados, peeled, pitted and cubed
1 Jerusalem artichoke, peeled and cut in matchstick pieces
2 papayas, peeled, halved lengthwise, seeded and sliced crosswise
Juice of 1 lemon
Juice of 1 lime
Fresh mint

Dressing:
2 tablespoons honey
¼ cup lime juice
½ cup extra virgin olive oil
Salt and pepper

1. Sprinkle avocados with lemon juice. In a separate bowl, toss Jerusalem artichoke with lime juice.

2. Combine honey, ¼ cup lime juice, and salt and pepper in a bowl. Add oil in a stream, whisking constantly until thoroughly combined.

3. Arrange papaya on a platter, mound avocado over it, and sprinkle with drained Jerusalem artichoke.

4. Drizzle the dressing over the salad and garnish with fresh mint.

POTTED SHRIMP

½ pound shrimp
⅔ cup clarified butter
　Nutmeg
　Cayenne pepper
　Salt

1. Shell and devein uncooked shrimp, reserving shells. In a heavy skillet, cook shells in butter over moderately low heat, stirring for 2 or 3 minutes or until shells are pink.

2. In a food processor fitted with steel blade, grind the shell mixture well, and strain it through a very fine sieve over a heavy skillet, pressing hard on the solids. Add the shrimp and cook over moderately low heat for 2 minutes or until shrimp turn pink.

3. Transfer shrimp and butter to food processor bowl. Add freshly grated nutmeg, cayenne and salt to taste. Blend the mixture until shrimp is ground fine, but not pureed.

4. Transfer mixture to a bowl and chill, covered for 1 hour or until firm.

5. Use as a spread for crusty French bread.

MIXED FRUIT BARS

1½ cups all-purpose flour
⅓ cup wheat germ
2 teaspoons baking powder
½ teaspoon salt
½ cup dates, chopped
½ cup dried figs, chopped
½ cup dried apricots, chopped
½ cup walnuts, chopped
3 tablespoons sesame seeds
3 eggs
½ cup vegetable oil
½ cup honey
1 teaspoon vanilla extract

Oven temperature: 325°

1. Mix flour, wheat germ, baking powder and salt in a large bowl. Stir in fruit, nuts and sesame seeds.

2. In another bowl combine eggs, oil, honey and vanilla. Add to dry ingredients and stir until just blended.

3. Spread mixture in a buttered 8-inch square baking dish. Bake 35 to 40 minutes or until cake tester inserted in the center comes out clean.

4. Cool and cut into 16 squares.

SHRIMP SALAD

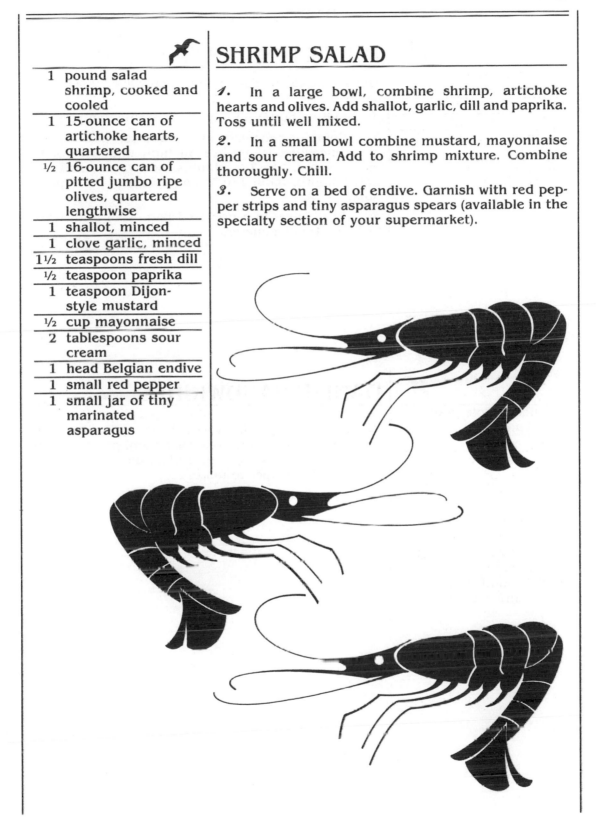

1	pound salad shrimp, cooked and cooled
1	15-ounce can of artichoke hearts, quartered
½	16-ounce can of pitted jumbo ripe olives, quartered lengthwise
1	shallot, minced
1	clove garlic, minced
1½	teaspoons fresh dill
½	teaspoon paprika
1	teaspoon Dijon-style mustard
½	cup mayonnaise
2	tablespoons sour cream
1	head Belgian endive
1	small red pepper
1	small jar of tiny marinated asparagus

1. In a large bowl, combine shrimp, artichoke hearts and olives. Add shallot, garlic, dill and paprika. Toss until well mixed.

2. In a small bowl combine mustard, mayonnaise and sour cream. Add to shrimp mixture. Combine thoroughly. Chill.

3. Serve on a bed of endive. Garnish with red pepper strips and tiny asparagus spears (available in the specialty section of your supermarket).

MILK CHOCOLATE FUDGE

12 ounces milk chocolate, chopped
¼ cup heavy cream
⅛ teaspoon salt
½ teaspoon vanilla extract
¾ cup walnuts, chopped

This recipe can be done in the microwave quickly and easily.

1. Lightly butter an 8-inch square baking pan.

2. Combine chocolate, cream and salt in a 1-quart glass measure. Microwave on high until chocolate melts, about 2 to 2½ minutes. Add vanilla and stir until smooth, about 2 to 3 minutes. Blend in chopped nuts.

3. Pour fudge into prepared pan. Cool until firm. Cut into 1-inch squares.

DANISH SANDWICHES

4 slices whole grain bread
4 slices ham
4 slices turkey
4 slices rare roast beef
¼ cup dill mayonnaise (see recipe)
1 Bermuda onion, thinly sliced and separated into rings
¼ cup capers
  Salt and freshly ground pepper

1. Spread bread slices with dill mayonnaise. Top each slice of bread with one slice ham, one slice turkey, one slice roast beef, several onion rings, capers, and salt and pepper to taste.

2. Serve sandwiches open-faced.

GERMAN-STYLE POTATO SALAD

2 large potatoes, peeled and quartered
4 slices bacon, diced
½ green pepper, chopped
1 tablespoon tarragon vinegar
1 tablespoon cider vinegar
1 tablespoon olive oil
Salt and pepper
Fresh tarragon

1. Cook potatoes in boiling water about 20 minutes, or until tender. Drain. Sprinkle with tarragon vinegar and cider vinegar. Toss.

2. Cook bacon. Pour diced bacon along with its fat over potatoes. Add green pepper, olive oil and salt and pepper to taste. Stir carefully to thoroughly combine ingredients. Cool.

3. To serve, reheat and garnish with fresh tarragon.

ALMOND-FILLED BROWNIES

4 eggs
2 cups granulated sugar
½ cup butter, melted
6 ounces unsweetened chocolate, melted
1 teaspoon vanilla extract
1 cup flour
½ teaspoon baking powder
½ teaspoon salt
½ cup sliced almonds (optional)

Almond Filling:
1 8-ounce can almond paste
1 egg
1 teaspoon almond extract

Oven temperature: 350°

1. Beat together eggs, sugar, butter and chocolate.

2. Add vanilla, flour, baking powder and salt, mixing after each addition.

3. To prepare almond filling: Combine all ingredients in a food processor fitted with the steel blade until thoroughly blended.

4. Pour half of chocolate mixture into a greased and floured 9" × 13" pan. Spread with almond filling and sprinkle with almonds. Pour remaining batter over all. Bake in a preheated oven for 25 minutes.

5. Let cool 45 minutes before cutting.

Yield: 24 brownies.

COLESLAW

½ pound green cabbage, shredded

½ pound red cabbage, shredded

1 medium carrot, shredded

½ medium onion, thinly sliced

½ cup vinegar

⅓ cup granulated sugar

¼ cup salad oil

½ teaspoon salt

½ teaspoon dry mustard

1. Toss green cabbage with red cabbage, carrots, and onion.

2. In a saucepan, bring to a boil vinegar, sugar, salad oil, salt and dry mustard.

3. Pour boiling vinegar mixture over cabbage mixture. Toss. Chill.

LEMON SQUARES

1 cup all-purpose flour

½ cup butter, softened

¼ cup confectioner's sugar

2 eggs

1 cup granulated sugar

½ teaspoon baking powder

½ teaspoon salt

2 teaspoons lemon peel, grated

2 tablespoons lemon juice

Confectioner's sugar to garnish

Oven temperature: 350°

1. Mix flour, butter and ¼ cup confectioner's sugar. Press in ungreased 8-inch square pan, building up ½-inch edges. Bake in preheated oven for 20 minutes.

2. Beat remaining ingredients until light and fluffy, about 3 minutes. Pour over hot crust. Bake 25 minutes or until center springs back when lightly touched.

3. Cool. Cut in squares. Sprinkle with confectioner's sugar.

Yield: 16 squares.

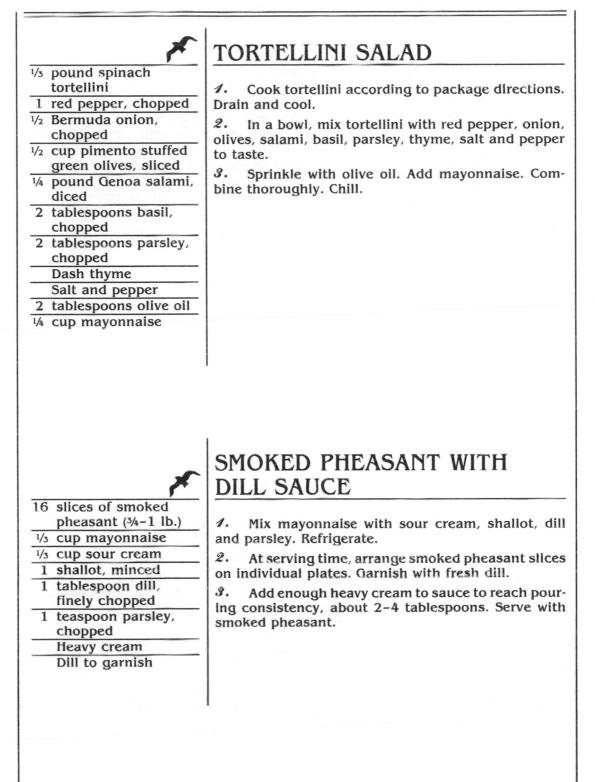

TORTELLINI SALAD

1/3 pound spinach tortellini

1 red pepper, chopped

1/2 Bermuda onion, chopped

1/2 cup pimento stuffed green olives, sliced

1/4 pound Genoa salami, diced

2 tablespoons basil, chopped

2 tablespoons parsley, chopped

Dash thyme

Salt and pepper

2 tablespoons olive oil

1/4 cup mayonnaise

1. Cook tortellini according to package directions. Drain and cool.

2. In a bowl, mix tortellini with red pepper, onion, olives, salami, basil, parsley, thyme, salt and pepper to taste.

3. Sprinkle with olive oil. Add mayonnaise. Combine thoroughly. Chill.

SMOKED PHEASANT WITH DILL SAUCE

16 slices of smoked pheasant (3/4–1 lb.)

1/3 cup mayonnaise

1/3 cup sour cream

1 shallot, minced

1 tablespoon dill, finely chopped

1 teaspoon parsley, chopped

Heavy cream

Dill to garnish

1. Mix mayonnaise with sour cream, shallot, dill and parsley. Refrigerate.

2. At serving time, arrange smoked pheasant slices on individual plates. Garnish with fresh dill.

3. Add enough heavy cream to sauce to reach pouring consistency, about 2–4 tablespoons. Serve with smoked pheasant.

CHEF'S SALAD WITH SHALLOT VINAIGRETTE

1 pound smoked beef tongue, cooked and trimmed

½ pound Jarlsberg cheese, diced

6 ounces Genoa salami

⅔ cup ripe olives

1 green pepper

1 red pepper

½ pound zucchini

½ pound carrots

5 cups romaine, shredded or torn

Shallot Vinaigrette:

½ cup lemon juice

2 teaspoons Dijon-style mustard

1 cup good quality olive oil

¼ cup shallots, finely minced

Salt and pepper

1. Cut meats and vegetables into julienne. Place lettuce on 4 salad plates. Arrange meats, cheese, olives and vegetables decoratively on the lettuce.

2. To prepare shallot vinaigrette: In a glass bowl, combine lemon juice and mustard. Add oil in a stream, whisking vigorously. Whisk until smooth.

3. Add shallots, and salt and pepper to taste.

4. Serve with Chef's Salad.

APRICOT POUND CAKE

1 cup unsalted butter, softened

3 cups granulated sugar

6 large eggs

1 cup sour cream

½ cup apricot brandy

1 teaspoon vanilla extract

2 teaspoons dark rum

3 cups all-purpose flour

½ teaspoon salt

½ teaspoon baking soda

Oven temperature: 325°

1. In a large bowl, cream butter and sugar. Beat until mixture is light and fluffy. Add eggs one at a time, beating well after each addition. Beat in sour cream, brandy, vanilla and rum.

2. In another bowl, sift together the flour, salt and baking soda. Stir the flour mixture into the butter and egg mixture.

3. Pour batter into a buttered bundt pan and bake for 1 hour, or until a cake tester inserted in the center comes out clean.

4. Cool the cake in the pan on a rack for 1 hour. Then, turn it out of the pan on rack to cool completely.

RYE MUFFINS

☐ 🐦🐦🐦

1½	teaspoons active dry yeast
¼	cup lukewarm water
1½	teaspoons light brown sugar
1½	cups, plus ⅓ cup all-purpose flour
¾	cup warm water
⅔	cup rye flour
2	teaspoons unsalted butter, melted
2	teaspoons unsulfured molasses
1½	teaspoons orange rind, grated
¾	teaspoon salt
¼	teaspoon cumin
1	egg, beaten

Oven temperature: 350°

1. In large mixer bowl, combine yeast, ¼ cup water, and brown sugar. Let set 15 minutes, or until foamy.

2. Add 1 cup all-purpose flour, ¾ cup warm water, rye flour, butter, molasses, orange rind, salt and cumin. Beat with electric mixer for 5 minutes. Beat in ½ cup more all-purpose flour. With a wooden spoon, stir in ⅓ cup all-purpose flour; stir until well combined. The dough will be sticky.

3. Let dough rise, covered with plastic wrap, 1½ hours or until doubled in bulk.

4. Stir down the dough with a tablespoon coated with vegetable oil. Spoon a rounded tablespoon of dough into each of 32 buttered muffin tin compartments. Press lightly into tins with oiled fingers and let the muffins rise, uncovered, for 20 minutes or until almost doubled. Brush the muffins with beaten egg and bake for 20 minutes or until golden brown. Turn muffins on a rack to cool.

NOTE: These are wonderful served warm. You may want to leave them in the sun for a while before serving.

CHICKEN & WATERCRESS SANDWICHES

🐦

8	slices oatmeal bread
	Tarragon mayonnaise (see recipe)
2	whole chicken breasts, cooked and thinly sliced
1	bunch watercress
	Salt and pepper

Spread bread slices with tarragon mayonnaise. Layer 4 slices of bread with slices of chicken. Arrange watercress leaves over chicken. Salt and pepper to taste. Top with remaining 4 slices of bread. Cut diagonally in quarters.

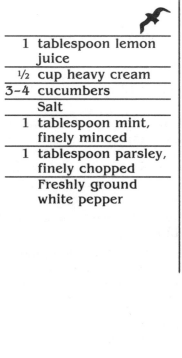

CUCUMBER MINT SALAD

1 tablespoon lemon
   juice
½ cup heavy cream
3–4 cucumbers
   Salt
1 tablespoon mint,
   finely minced
1 tablespoon parsley,
   finely chopped
   Freshly ground
   white pepper

1. In a bowl, combine lemon juice and cream. Let mixture stand for 2 to 3 hours.

2. Peel cucumbers and cut them in half lengthwise. Remove the seeds. Cut cucumbers into ¼-inch slices. Sprinkle with salt and let them stand in a sieve over a bowl for 30 minutes.

3. Dry cucumbers on a paper towel. Combine with cream mixture. Sprinkle with mint, parsley, salt and pepper. Chill.

NOTE: Cucumbers may be prepared one day ahead of time, but they will lose some of their crispness.

DATE PINWHEELS

1 cup butter
2 cups light brown
   sugar
3 eggs, well beaten
4 cups flour
½ teaspoon salt
½ teaspoon baking
   soda

Date Filling:
2¼ cups dates,
   chopped
1 cup granulated
   sugar
1 cup water
1 cup nuts, chopped

Oven temperature: 400°

1. Cream butter with brown sugar. Stir in eggs.

2. Sift together dry ingredients. Add to creamed butter and mix well. Chill.

3. Prepare date filling: In saucepan, combine dates, sugar and water. Bring to a boil and cook over medium heat for 10 minutes or until thick. Add chopped nuts. Cool.

4. Divide dough into two parts. Roll into rectangles ¼-inch thick. Spread with date filling. Roll up beginning with long side. Wrap in waxed paper and chill overnight.

5. Cut in ½-inch slices and arrange flat on baking sheet.

6. Bake 10 minutes or until firm.

Yield: 60 cookies.

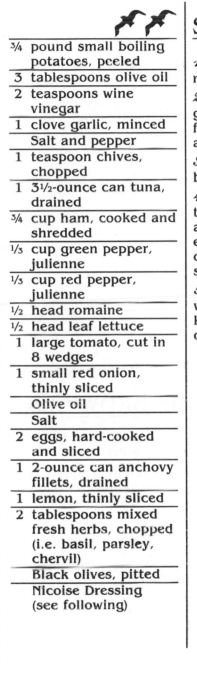

3/4 pound small boiling potatoes, peeled

3 tablespoons olive oil

2 teaspoons wine vinegar

1 clove garlic, minced

Salt and pepper

1 teaspoon chives, chopped

1 3½-ounce can tuna, drained

3/4 cup ham, cooked and shredded

1/3 cup green pepper, julienne

1/3 cup red pepper, julienne

1/2 head romaine

1/2 head leaf lettuce

1 large tomato, cut in 8 wedges

1 small red onion, thinly sliced

Olive oil

Salt

2 eggs, hard-cooked and sliced

1 2-ounce can anchovy fillets, drained

1 lemon, thinly sliced

2 tablespoons mixed fresh herbs, chopped (i.e. basil, parsley, chervil)

Black olives, pitted

Nicoise Dressing (see following)

SALAD NICOISE

1. Cook potatoes in boiling, salted water for 15 minutes, or until just tender. Cool slightly. Slice.

2. Combine 3 tablespoons olive oil, vinegar and garlic in medium bowl. Add potatoes and stir carefully to coat each slice. Season with salt and pepper and sprinkle with chives.

3. Combine tuna, ham, and peppers in a small bowl. Cover with half of Nicoise dressing.

4. Arrange romaine and lettuce on a platter. Place tuna mixture in center. Spread remaining dressing around the edge of the platter. Place potatoes on one end. Arrange tomatoes next to potatoes. Arrange onion rings over tomatoes. Drizzle with olive oil and sprinkle with salt.

5. Place eggs at opposite end of platter; crisscross with anchovy strips. Garnish with lemon slices. Sprinkle the entire salad with fresh herbs and garnish with olives.

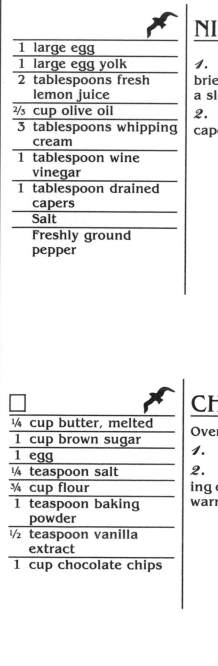

NICOISE DRESSING

1 large egg
1 large egg yolk
2 tablespoons fresh lemon juice
⅔ cup olive oil
3 tablespoons whipping cream
1 tablespoon wine vinegar
1 tablespoon drained capers
Salt
Freshly ground pepper

1. Place egg and additional egg yolk in blender. Mix briefly. Blend in lemon juice. With motor on, add oil in a slow, steady stream.

2. Transfer to a small bowl. Mix in cream, vinegar, capers, salt and pepper. Set aside.

CHOCOLATE CHIP BROWNIES

¼ cup butter, melted
1 cup brown sugar
1 egg
¼ teaspoon salt
¾ cup flour
1 teaspoon baking powder
½ teaspoon vanilla extract
1 cup chocolate chips

Oven temperature: 350°

1. Mix ingredients together in order.

2. Spread mixture in a buttered 8-inch square baking dish. Bake 25 minutes. Cut into squares while still warm.

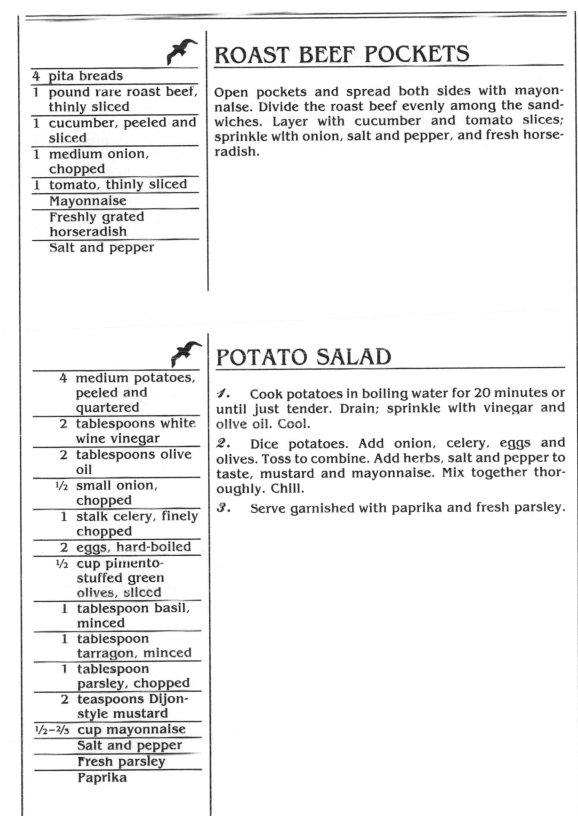

ROAST BEEF POCKETS

4 pita breads

1 pound rare roast beef, thinly sliced

1 cucumber, peeled and sliced

1 medium onion, chopped

1 tomato, thinly sliced

Mayonnaise

Freshly grated horseradish

Salt and pepper

Open pockets and spread both sides with mayonnaise. Divide the roast beef evenly among the sandwiches. Layer with cucumber and tomato slices; sprinkle with onion, salt and pepper, and fresh horseradish.

POTATO SALAD

4 medium potatoes, peeled and quartered

2 tablespoons white wine vinegar

2 tablespoons olive oil

1/2 small onion, chopped

1 stalk celery, finely chopped

2 eggs, hard-boiled

1/2 cup pimento-stuffed green olives, sliced

1 tablespoon basil, minced

1 tablespoon tarragon, minced

1 tablespoon parsley, chopped

2 teaspoons Dijon-style mustard

1/2–2/3 cup mayonnaise

Salt and pepper

Fresh parsley

Paprika

1. Cook potatoes in boiling water for 20 minutes or until just tender. Drain; sprinkle with vinegar and olive oil. Cool.

2. Dice potatoes. Add onion, celery, eggs and olives. Toss to combine. Add herbs, salt and pepper to taste, mustard and mayonnaise. Mix together thoroughly. Chill.

3. Serve garnished with paprika and fresh parsley.

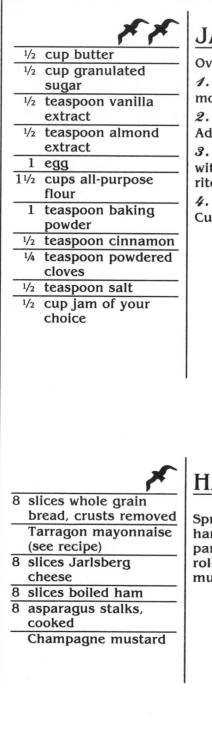

JAM BARS

Oven temperature: 400°

1.   Cream together butter, sugar, vanilla and almond extracts. Stir in egg.

2.   In another bowl, sift together dry ingredients. Add to first mixture and blend well.

3.   Butter an 8-inch square baking dish and spread with half the mixture. Cover with a layer of your favorite jam. Spread the rest of the dough on top.

4.   Bake 25 minutes or until lightly browned. Cool. Cut in bars.

½	cup butter
½	cup granulated sugar
½	teaspoon vanilla extract
½	teaspoon almond extract
1	egg
1½	cups all-purpose flour
1	teaspoon baking powder
½	teaspoon cinnamon
¼	teaspoon powdered cloves
½	teaspoon salt
½	cup jam of your choice

HAM & CHEESE ROLL-UPS

Spread bread slices with tarragon mayonnaise. Divide ham and cheese among slices of bread. Place an asparagus stalk at one end of each slice of bread and roll tightly. Secure with toothpicks. Use Champagne mustard for dipping sauce.

8	slices whole grain bread, crusts removed
	Tarragon mayonnaise (see recipe)
8	slices Jarlsberg cheese
8	slices boiled ham
8	asparagus stalks, cooked
	Champagne mustard

FOOD PROCESSOR MAYONNAISE

1 whole egg
2 egg yolks
¼ teaspoon dry mustard
1 teaspoon salt
2 tablespoons wine vinegar
2 cups good quality olive oil, salad oil, or a combination of the two

1.   Using the metal blade, process the egg, yolks, mustard and salt for 1 minute. Add vinegar; blend. Add oil in a thin stream of droplets.

2.   Correct seasonings. Store in a covered container in the refrigerator.

NOTE: The above mayonnaise has many uses as a plain mayonnaise. For variety, add tarragon (about 1 tablespoon), garlic, dill, or other herbs to taste in step #1.

CHILLED ZUCCHINI SOUP

4 small zucchini, cut in 1-inch cubes
1½ tablespoons olive oil
1½ tablespoons unsalted butter
2 small onions, finely minced
1 clove garlic, finely minced
3¾ cups chicken stock
1½ tablespoons fresh parsley, chives, and basil, mixed
1 teaspoon lemon juice
Salt
Freshly ground black pepper
½ cup heavy cream
¾ cup sour cream, mixed with chives

1.   Salt zucchini cubes and place them in a sieve over a bowl for at least 30 minutes to drain.

2.   In a large, flame-proof casserole, heat olive oil and butter. Add onion and garlic and cook over low heat for 5 minutes. Do not brown.

3.   Rinse and dry the zucchini cubes well on paper towels. Add to casserole and continue cooking over low heat for 5 minutes.

4.   Add chicken stock and let simmer for 15 minutes. Turn off heat. When soup is cool enough, puree in blender. Do not try to puree *hot* soup.

5.   Add herbs, lemon juice, salt and pepper. Chill.

6.   Just before serving, add cream. Garnish with sour cream and chives.

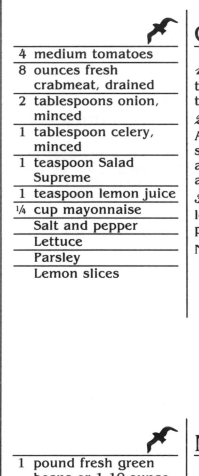

CRABMEAT STUFFED TOMATOES

4 medium tomatoes
8 ounces fresh crabmeat, drained
2 tablespoons onion, minced
1 tablespoon celery, minced
1 teaspoon Salad Supreme
1 teaspoon lemon juice
¼ cup mayonnaise
Salt and pepper
Lettuce
Parsley
Lemon slices

1. Rinse tomatoes, remove stem and cut into quarters ⅔ to ¾ of the way through, so sections are attached at the base.

2. In a bowl, separate crabmeat into small pieces. Add onion, celery, Salad Supreme (available in the spice section of your local supermarket), lemon juice, and salt and pepper to taste; toss. Add mayonnaise and combine thoroughly. Chill.

3. Place tomatoes on individual plates on lettuce leaves. Fill with crabmeat mixture. Garnish with fresh parsley and lemon slices.

NOTE: The tomatoes and crabmeat may be prepared ahead and transported separately for quick assembly on board. They do not travel as well when they are assembled ahead of time.

MARINATED GREEN BEANS

1 pound fresh green beans or 1 10-ounce package frozen whole green beans
3 tablespoons white wine vinegar
⅓ cup olive oil
2 teaspoons dill, finely chopped
Salt and pepper

1. Cut ends from fresh green beans and cook in boiling water for 5 minutes or until just tender (beans should be slightly crisp), or cook according to package directions. Cool.

2. Mix wine vinegar with dill; salt and pepper to taste. Whisk in olive oil until mixture is well combined. Pour over beans. Chill.

3. Serve garnished with additional fresh dill.

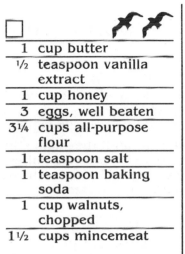

1	cup butter
½	teaspoon vanilla extract
1	cup honey
3	eggs, well beaten
3¼	cups all-purpose flour
1	teaspoon salt
1	teaspoon baking soda
1	cup walnuts, chopped
1½	cups mincemeat

MINCEMEAT COOKIES

Oven temperature: 350°

1. Cream butter; beat in vanilla, honey and eggs.

2. Sift together flour, salt and soda. Mix with butter and egg mixture. Stir in walnuts and mincemeat.

3. Arrange by teaspoonsful on a buttered baking sheet. Bake 15 minutes or until lightly brown.

Yield: 75 cookies.

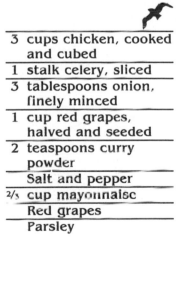

3	cups chicken, cooked and cubed
1	stalk celery, sliced
3	tablespoons onion, finely minced
1	cup red grapes, halved and seeded
2	teaspoons curry powder
	Salt and pepper
⅔	cup mayonnaise
	Red grapes
	Parsley

CURRIED CHICKEN SALAD

1. Toss chicken with celery, onion, grapes, curry powder and salt and pepper to taste. Add mayonnaise to moisten. Chill.

2. Serve garnished with red grapes and parsley.

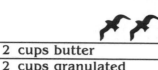

CHOCOLATE CHIP POUND CAKE

2 cups butter

2 cups granulated sugar

10 eggs, separated

1 teaspoon vanilla extract

1 teaspoon salt

12 ounces chocolate chips

1 teaspoon cream of tartar

4 cups all-purpose flour

Oven temperature: 325°

1. Grease a 10-inch tube pan.

2. Cream together butter and ¼ cup sugar, until mixture is light and fluffy. Add egg yolks, one at a time, beating well after each addition. Stir in vanilla.

3. Add salt to egg whites. Beat until they hold stiff peaks. Add the remaining sugar to the egg whites, one tablespoon at a time, beating well after each addition. Continue beating until egg whites are very stiff.

4. Sift flour together with cream of tartar.

5. Gently fold beaten egg whites and flour alternately into creamed butter mixture. Fold in chocolate chips.

6. Pour batter into prepared pan. Bake in a preheated oven until golden brown, about 1 hour and 50 minutes.

4

THE WEEKEND SAIL

*T*hough an overnight is a treat, a weekend out is like a mini-vacation. It's just enough time to relax and refresh before the busy days ahead. Life in the everyday world comes to an abrupt halt; the pace slows as we revel in the heat of the summer. There is a oneness with nature whether drifting along or beating hard into the wind. You feel at once both the challenge and the soothing that is nature.

When I'm especially organized, we embark Friday, late afternoon or early evening, and sail to a nearby cove for dinner; when I'm not, we set out Saturday after breakfast. The days run much as they would if we were just out for an overnight. We simply have the luxury of extending the time—a luxury that allows us to completely strip away the tensions of the work world.

Menus for this section begin with Friday dinner and end with Sunday brunch. Within this framework, there is lots of leeway for as much or as little preparation as fits into your schedule and your mood. Weekend sails are a good time to delegate responsibility, giving a whole meal over to another person or couple to prepare. I find this works better than sharing in each meal's preparation; this way we each get a few meals where we are completely carefree.

MENU ✦ I

Friday Dinner

★ Shrimp with Tomatoes and Feta Cheese ★
Brown Rice with Parsley
Buttered Kale
★ Sourdough French Rolls/Butter ★
★ Amaretto Cheesecake Cookies ★

Saturday Breakfast

Grapefruit Half
★ Magnifique Eggs ★
Bacon (cook ahead at home in microwave, reheat on board)
Coffee

Saturday Lunch

★ Seafood Salad ★
★ Endive and Grapefruit Salad ★
French Bread/Butter
★ Shortbread/Fresh Fruit (see page 103) ★

Saturday Dinner

★ Grilled Pork Tenderloin ★
★ Lyonnaise Potatoes ★
Snow Peas with Waterchestnuts
★ Chocolate Cake with Raspberries & Chocolate Sauce ★

Sunday Brunch

Cassaba Melon with Prosciutto
★ Broccoli and Ham Quiche ★
★ Oatmeal Banana Muffins/Butter ★
Coffee/Tea

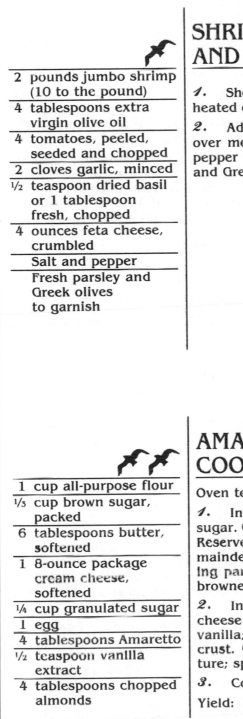

SHRIMP WITH TOMATOES AND FETA CHEESE

2 pounds jumbo shrimp
(10 to the pound)

4 tablespoons extra
virgin olive oil

4 tomatoes, peeled,
seeded and chopped

2 cloves garlic, minced

½ teaspoon dried basil
or 1 tablespoon
fresh, chopped

4 ounces feta cheese,
crumbled

Salt and pepper

Fresh parsley and
Greek olives
to garnish

1. Shell and devein the raw shrimp. Sauté shrimp in heated oil for 5 to 6 minutes or until they turn pink.

2. Add tomatoes, garlic, basil and the cheese. Stir over medium heat for another 5 minutes. Salt and pepper to taste. Serve garnished with fresh parsley and Greek olives.

AMARETTO CHEESECAKE COOKIES

1 cup all-purpose flour

⅓ cup brown sugar,
packed

6 tablespoons butter,
softened

1 8-ounce package
cream cheese,
softened

¼ cup granulated sugar

1 egg

4 tablespoons Amaretto

½ teaspoon vanilla
extract

4 tablespoons chopped
almonds

Oven temperature: 350°

1. In a large mixing bowl, combine flour and brown sugar. Cut in butter until mixture forms fine crumbs. Reserve 1 cup crumb mixture for topping. Press remainder over bottom of ungreased 8-inch square baking pan. Bake for 12 to 15 minutes or until lightly browned.

2. In mixer bowl, thoroughly cream together cream cheese and granulated sugar. Add egg, Amaretto and vanilla; beat well. Spread batter over partially baked crust. Combine almonds with reserved crumb mixture; sprinkle over batter. Bake for 20–25 minutes.

3. Cool and cut into squares.

Yield: 16 cookies.

SOURDOUGH FRENCH ROLLS

Oven temperature: 375°

1. To prepare starter, place milk in a glass jar. Let it stand for 24 hours at room temperature. Stir in flour. Leave mixture uncovered in a warm place for 3 days or until bubbly and sour.

2. To prepare rolls: In a large mixing bowl combine first four ingredients. Stir until mixture is dissolved and completely blended. Add flour and mix well. Turn out onto a lightly floured board. Turn dough over several times until it handles easily and is smooth and elastic. Place in a greased bowl, cover with a clean cloth, and let rise in a warm place for 2 hours.

3. Punch dough down and knead about 20 times until all air is removed from the dough. (Use a rolling pin to press out the air.) Roll the dough into an oblong shape 12″ × 16″. Starting with the long side, roll up the dough, sealing the edges. Seal very well and cut into 12 equal slices.

4. Place in a greased baking pan that has been sprinkled with cornmeal. Brush top of the rolls with water. Again, let rise for about 90 minutes in a warm place.

5. Preheat oven to 375°. Bake for 15–20 minutes. The rolls should be golden brown. Remove from oven to cooling rack.

Ingredients (Sourdough French Rolls):

- 1 cup sourdough starter
- 1 cup lukewarm water
- 1 tablespoon butter, melted
- 1½ teaspoons salt
- 4 cups all-purpose flour
- ½ teaspoon baking soda

Sourdough Starter:

- 1 cup milk
- 1 cup flour

MAGNIFIQUE EGGS

1. Fill a 10-inch skillet about ¾ full with water. Add salt. Bring to boil. Break 8 eggs into bowl or pie plate. Add eggs to boiling water and simmer for 3 to 5 minutes, until whites are cooked and yolks are still soft.

2. Meanwhile, in a saucepan, over low heat, blend additional 4 egg yolks with orange juice and salt. Add butter, ½ stick at a time, and mix after each addition with wire whisk until blended. When all the butter has been added, cook, stirring constantly until thickened.

3. Place three asparagus spears on each English muffin half, top with a poached egg (use slotted spoon to remove from skillet) and spoon orange hollandaise over all. Garnish with fresh watercress.

Ingredients (Magnifique Eggs):

- 8 eggs
- 4 egg yolks
- 2 tablespoons orange juice
- ¼ teaspoon salt
- 1 cup butter
- 24 asparagus spears, cooked
- 4 English muffins, toasted and buttered
- Fresh watercress to garnish

SEAFOOD SALAD

Shrimp, cooked
Scallops, cooked
Crabmeat, cooked
Scallions, chopped
Fresh parsley, minced
Fresh tarragon, minced
Sherry
Mayonnaise
Salt and white pepper
Avocado slices and cherry tomatoes to garnish

1. Cut shrimp, scallops and crabmeat into bite-sized chunks. Combine all ingredients together in a bowl. Chill.

2. Serve with avocado slices and cherry tomatoes.

ENDIVE & GRAPEFRUIT SALAD

4 heads endive
1 large grapefruit
French dressing
Parsley

1. Trim and rinse endive. Separate the leaves, pat dry with a towel, and chill.

2. Cut rind and white pith from grapefruit. Separate into sections and chill.

3. Just before serving arrange endive and grapefruit on a platter and sprinkle with French dressing. Garnish with parsley.

GRILLED PORK TENDERLOIN IN WINE MARINADE

2 pounds pork tenderloin
½ cup red wine
½ cup oil
2–3 garlic cloves, split
1 teaspoon dried herbs (thyme, rosemary, marjoram)
2 tablespoons fresh parsley, finely chopped
¼ cup onion, chopped
Freshly ground pepper to taste

1. Mix together all ingredients except tenderloin. Pour over pork tenderloin.

2. Marinate pork 4 hours, or overnight.

3. Grill over hot coals 10 minutes, or until it reaches desired degree of doneness. Baste occasionally with marinade.

Marinate: 4 hours or overnight.

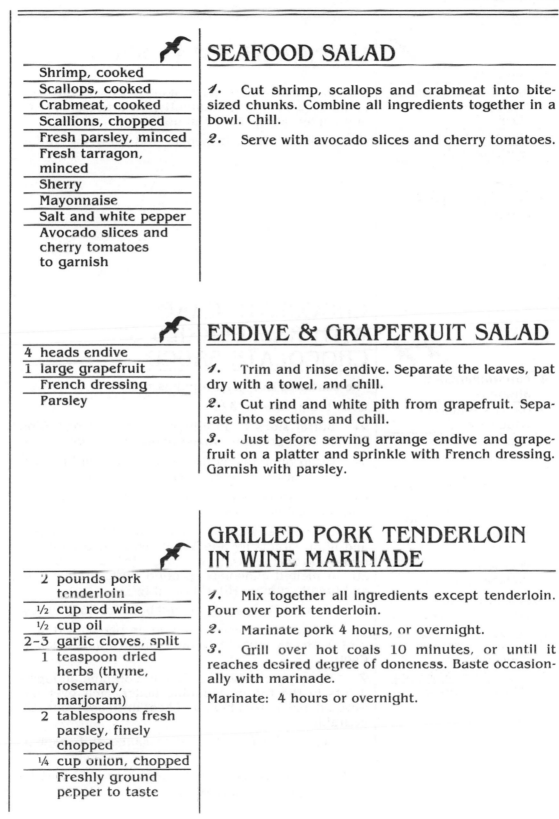

LYONNAISE POTATOES

1. In hot butter in a large skillet, sauté potato and onion slices, turning frequently, until golden brown and tender, about 20–25 minutes.

2. Sprinkle with salt, pepper and parsley.

¼ cup butter
4 medium potatoes, peeled and thinly sliced
1 cup onion, sliced
1 teaspoon salt
Pepper, freshly ground
2 tablespoons parsley, chopped

CHOCOLATE CAKE WITH RASPBERRIES & CHOCOLATE SAUCE

The center of this cake remains moist!

Oven temperature: 375°

1. Butter sides of an 8-inch round cake pan. Line bottom with buttered waxed paper. Set aside.

2. Grind almonds as fine as possible (without becoming a paste) in food processor. Set aside.

3. Melt chocolate in the top of a double boiler over hot, not boiling, water.

4. Beat butter with an electric mixer until very soft and light. Gradually add sugar, beating constantly. Add eggs, one at a time, beating after each addition. Stir in melted chocolate, ground nuts, orange rind and bread crumbs. Mix thoroughly.

5. Pour into prepared pan and bake for 25 minutes.

6. Remove from oven and cool in pan for 30 minutes. Turn cake out onto a rack. Discard waxed paper. Cool.

7. To prepare Chocolate Sauce: Combine all ingredients in the top of a double boiler. Melt over hot water. Remove from heat and beat until cool, but still pourable.

8. Serve cake with chocolate sauce and raspberries.

NOTE: Sauce may be cooled completely and reheated to pouring consistency.

1 cup unblanched almonds
4 ounces semisweet chocolate
½ cup butter, room temperature, cut in pieces
⅔ cup granulated sugar
3 eggs
Grated rind of 1 large orange
¼ cup bread crumbs, very fine
Raspberries

Chocolate Sauce:
2 ounces unsweetened chocolate
2 ounces semisweet chocolate
¼ cup butter, softened
2 teaspoons honey

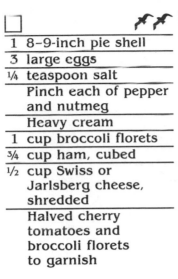

1 8–9-inch pie shell
3 large eggs
¼ teaspoon salt
   Pinch each of pepper
   and nutmeg
   Heavy cream
1 cup broccoli florets
¾ cup ham, cubed
½ cup Swiss or
   Jarlsberg cheese,
   shredded
   Halved cherry
   tomatoes and
   broccoli florets
   to garnish

BROCCOLI & HAM QUICHE

Oven temperature: 375°

1. Break eggs into a 4-cup measure. Add seasonings and beat together with eggs. Add cream to measure 1¾ cups; beat until well combined. Add remaining ingredients; mix thoroughly.

2. Pour into prepared pie shell and bake for 35 minutes.

3. Garnish with cherry tomato halves and additional broccoli florets.

⅓ cup granulated
   sugar
½ cup butter
2 eggs
3 medium bananas,
   mashed
¾ cup honey
1½ cups all-purpose
   flour
1 teaspoon baking
   powder
1 teaspoon baking
   soda
¾ teaspoon salt
1 cup quick-cooking
   rolled oats

OATMEAL BANANA MUFFINS

Oven temperature: 375°

1. In large mixer bowl, cream together sugar and butter. Beat in eggs, bananas and honey.

2. In another bowl, sift together flour, baking powder, soda and salt. Add to creamed mixture, beating until just blended. Stir in oats.

3. Line muffin pans with 24 paper baking cups, and fill to ⅔ with batter. Bake for 18–20 minutes.

4. Remove muffins from pans and cool on wire rack.

Yield: 24 muffins.

MENU • II

Friday Dinner

★ Flank Steak in Red Wine Marinade ★

★ Twice Baked Potatoes ★

★ Zucchini and Tomato Salad ★

★ Sherry Mushroom Sauté ★

★ Carrot Cake ★

Saturday Breakfast

★ Fresh Fruit Compote ★

★ Raisin Bran Muffins ★

Coffee/Tea

Saturday Lunch

★ Steak and Cheese Sandwiches ★

★ Vegetable Cottage Cheese ★

★ Special Oatmeal Raisin Cookies ★

Saturday Dinner

★ Oven Fried Chicken ★

★ Pasta Primavera ★

★ Spinach Salad ★

★ Chocolate Walnut Upside Down Cake ★

Sunday Brunch

Vanilla Yogurt with Fresh Fruit

★ Bacon and Cheese Omelet ★

★ Cheese Danish ★

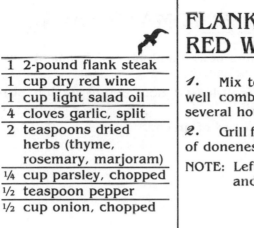

FLANK STEAK IN RED WINE MARINADE

1 2-pound flank steak
1 cup dry red wine
1 cup light salad oil
4 cloves garlic, split
2 teaspoons dried herbs (thyme, rosemary, marjoram)
¼ cup parsley, chopped
½ teaspoon pepper
½ cup onion, chopped

1.   Mix together all ingredients except steak until well combined. Add flank steak and marinate for several hours or overnight.

2.   Grill flank steak over hot coals to desired degree of doneness.

NOTE: Leftovers may be used for Saturday lunch's and cheese sandwiches.

TWICE BAKED POTATOES

4 medium baking potatoes
1 teaspoon Salad Supreme
¼ cup butter
¼ cup heavy cream
½ cup cheddar cheese, shredded
Salt and pepper
Paprika

1.   Bake potatoes at 400° for one hour.

2.   Thinly slice the top off each potato, lengthwise, and scoop out the pulp into a bowl.

3.   To the potato, add Salad Supreme (available in the spice section of your local supermarket), butter, cream, cheese, salt and pepper. Beat thoroughly until ingredients are well combined and there are no lumps.

4.   Spoon potato into hollowed-out skins. Sprinkle with paprika.

5.   Before serving, bring to room temperature and heat in a 350° oven for 25 minutes.

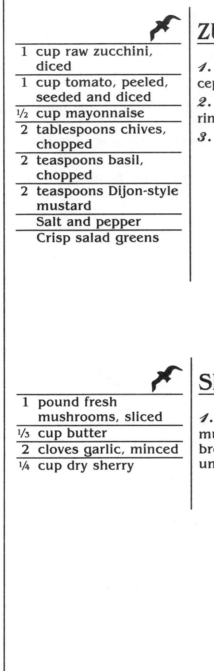

ZUCCHINI & TOMATO SALAD

1 cup raw zucchini, diced
1 cup tomato, peeled, seeded and diced
½ cup mayonnaise
2 tablespoons chives, chopped
2 teaspoons basil, chopped
2 teaspoons Dijon-style mustard
Salt and pepper
Crisp salad greens

1. In a medium bowl, combine all ingredients, except greens; mix gently.

2. Refrigerate at least 1 hour before serving, stirring occasionally.

3. Serve on a bed of greens.

SHERRY MUSHROOM SAUTÉ

1 pound fresh mushrooms, sliced
⅓ cup butter
2 cloves garlic, minced
¼ cup dry sherry

1. Heat butter in a large skillet. Add garlic and mushrooms. Sauté quickly until mushrooms are browned. Add sherry. Cook over high heat, stirring until sherry is reduced. Serve immediately.

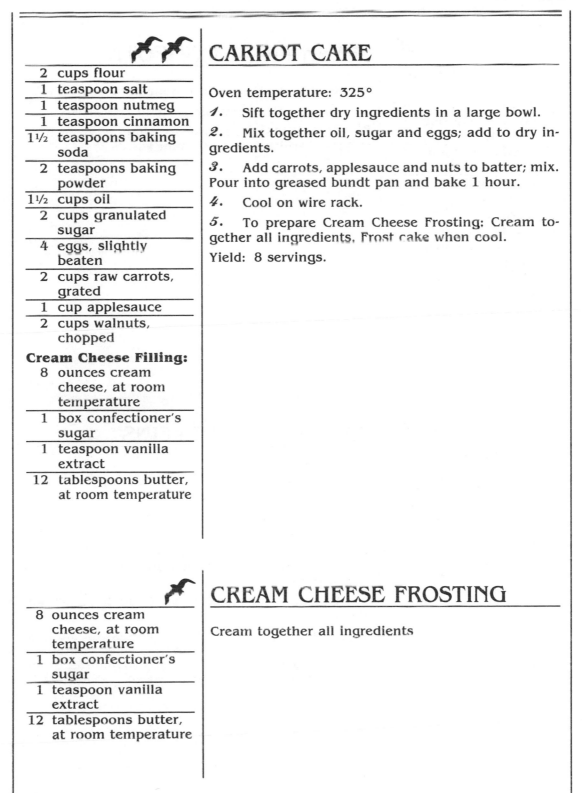

CARROT CAKE

2	cups flour
1	teaspoon salt
1	teaspoon nutmeg
1	teaspoon cinnamon
1½	teaspoons baking soda
2	teaspoons baking powder
1½	cups oil
2	cups granulated sugar
4	eggs, slightly beaten
2	cups raw carrots, grated
1	cup applesauce
2	cups walnuts, chopped

Cream Cheese Filling:

8	ounces cream cheese, at room temperature
1	box confectioner's sugar
1	teaspoon vanilla extract
12	tablespoons butter, at room temperature

Oven temperature: 325°

1. Sift together dry ingredients in a large bowl.

2. Mix together oil, sugar and eggs; add to dry ingredients.

3. Add carrots, applesauce and nuts to batter; mix. Pour into greased bundt pan and bake 1 hour.

4. Cool on wire rack.

5. To prepare Cream Cheese Frosting: Cream together all ingredients. Frost cake when cool.

Yield: 8 servings.

CREAM CHEESE FROSTING

8	ounces cream cheese, at room temperature
1	box confectioner's sugar
1	teaspoon vanilla extract
12	tablespoons butter, at room temperature

Cream together all ingredients

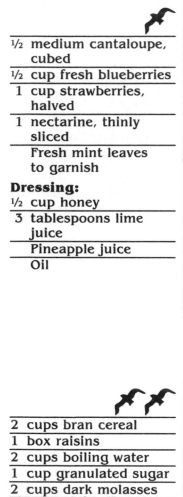

FRESH FRUIT COMPOTE

½ medium cantaloupe, cubed
½ cup fresh blueberries
1 cup strawberries, halved
1 nectarine, thinly sliced
Fresh mint leaves to garnish

Dressing:
½ cup honey
3 tablespoons lime juice
Pineapple juice
Oil

1. Gently combine fruit in a medium bowl. Chill.

2. Mix together remaining ingredients.

3. Lightly toss fruit with dressing. Serve in wine glasses. Garnish with fresh mint leaves.

RAISIN BRAN MUFFINS

2 cups bran cereal
1 box raisins
2 cups boiling water
1 cup granulated sugar
2 cups dark molasses
4 eggs, well beaten
1 quart buttermilk
3 cups bran cereal
5 cups flour
5 teaspoons baking soda
1 teaspoon salt

Oven temperature: 400°

1. Combine 2 cups bran cereal and raisins. Add 2 cups boiling water. Set aside to cool.

2. Mix together, in order, sugar, molasses, eggs, buttermilk, 3 cups bran cereal.

3. In a separate bowl combine flour, baking soda and salt; add to buttermilk mixture. Mix in the cooled raisin-bran mixture.

4. Fill paper-lined muffin tins ⅔ full. Bake 20 minutes.

NOTE: This recipe is enough for 4–5 dozen muffins. The mix may be stored in covered containers in the refrigerator for up to two months, or the muffins may be baked, frozen and reheated.

STEAK & CHEESE SANDWICHES

Leftover flank steak, thinly sliced (see page 65)

Red onion, thinly sliced

Boursin cheese

8 slices deli rye or pumpernickel

Mayonnaise

Salt and pepper

Bib lettuce

Dill spears to garnish

Spread 4 slices of bread with mayonnaise; spread the remaining four slices with boursin. Add steak, onion, salt and pepper, lettuce, and top slices of bread. Cut in two; serve with dill spears.

VEGETABLE COTTAGE CHEESE

1 pound cottage cheese

½ red pepper, chopped

1 carrot, chopped

1 stalk celery, thinly sliced

½ cup chives, chopped

Salad greens

Combine all ingredients, except greens. Serve atop a bed of greens.

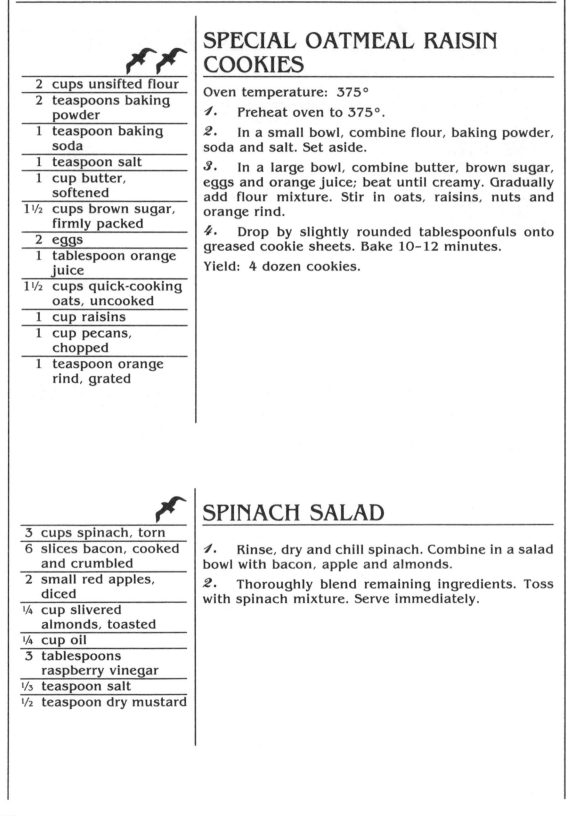

SPECIAL OATMEAL RAISIN COOKIES

2 cups unsifted flour
2 teaspoons baking powder
1 teaspoon baking soda
1 teaspoon salt
1 cup butter, softened
1½ cups brown sugar, firmly packed
2 eggs
1 tablespoon orange juice
1½ cups quick-cooking oats, uncooked
1 cup raisins
1 cup pecans, chopped
1 teaspoon orange rind, grated

Oven temperature: 375°

1. Preheat oven to 375°.

2. In a small bowl, combine flour, baking powder, soda and salt. Set aside.

3. In a large bowl, combine butter, brown sugar, eggs and orange juice; beat until creamy. Gradually add flour mixture. Stir in oats, raisins, nuts and orange rind.

4. Drop by slightly rounded tablespoonfuls onto greased cookie sheets. Bake 10–12 minutes.

Yield: 4 dozen cookies.

SPINACH SALAD

3 cups spinach, torn
6 slices bacon, cooked and crumbled
2 small red apples, diced
¼ cup slivered almonds, toasted
¼ cup oil
3 tablespoons raspberry vinegar
⅓ teaspoon salt
½ teaspoon dry mustard

1. Rinse, dry and chill spinach. Combine in a salad bowl with bacon, apple and almonds.

2. Thoroughly blend remaining ingredients. Toss with spinach mixture. Serve immediately.

OVEN FRIED CHICKEN

1 2½–3-pound fryer, cut into eighths
¼ cup Dijon-style mustard
¼ cup sour cream
Salt and pepper
1 cup cornflake crumbs or bread crumbs

Oven temperature: 350°

1. Wash chicken and pat dry.

2. Salt and pepper to taste. Spread with mustard, then sour cream. Coat with crumbs.

3. Spread out on baking sheet. Bake in a 350° oven for 1 hour.

PASTA PRIMAVERA

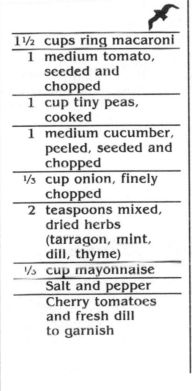

1½ cups ring macaroni
1 medium tomato, seeded and chopped
1 cup tiny peas, cooked
1 medium cucumber, peeled, seeded and chopped
⅓ cup onion, finely chopped
2 teaspoons mixed, dried herbs (tarragon, mint, dill, thyme)
⅓ cup mayonnaise
Salt and pepper
Cherry tomatoes and fresh dill to garnish

1. Cook macaroni according to package directions. Rinse, drain and cool.

2. Toss pasta with next four ingredients. Add herbs and salt and pepper. Combine with mayonnaise. Chill. Garnish with cherry tomatoes and fresh dill.

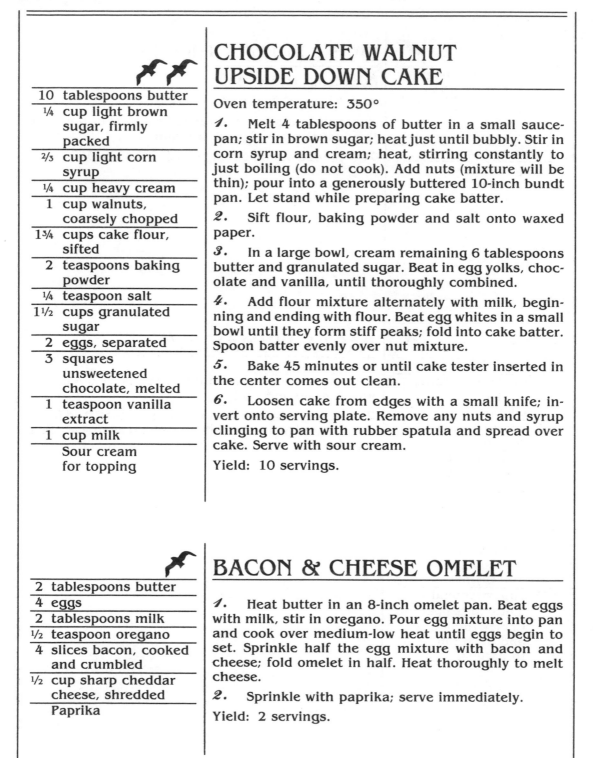

CHOCOLATE WALNUT UPSIDE DOWN CAKE

10	tablespoons butter
¼	cup light brown sugar, firmly packed
⅔	cup light corn syrup
¼	cup heavy cream
1	cup walnuts, coarsely chopped
1¾	cups cake flour, sifted
2	teaspoons baking powder
¼	teaspoon salt
1½	cups granulated sugar
2	eggs, separated
3	squares unsweetened chocolate, melted
1	teaspoon vanilla extract
1	cup milk
	Sour cream for topping

Oven temperature: 350°

1.   Melt 4 tablespoons of butter in a small saucepan; stir in brown sugar; heat just until bubbly. Stir in corn syrup and cream; heat, stirring constantly to just boiling (do not cook). Add nuts (mixture will be thin); pour into a generously buttered 10-inch bundt pan. Let stand while preparing cake batter.

2.   Sift flour, baking powder and salt onto waxed paper.

3.   In a large bowl, cream remaining 6 tablespoons butter and granulated sugar. Beat in egg yolks, chocolate and vanilla, until thoroughly combined.

4.   Add flour mixture alternately with milk, beginning and ending with flour. Beat egg whites in a small bowl until they form stiff peaks; fold into cake batter. Spoon batter evenly over nut mixture.

5.   Bake 45 minutes or until cake tester inserted in the center comes out clean.

6.   Loosen cake from edges with a small knife; invert onto serving plate. Remove any nuts and syrup clinging to pan with rubber spatula and spread over cake. Serve with sour cream.

Yield: 10 servings.

BACON & CHEESE OMELET

2	tablespoons butter
4	eggs
2	tablespoons milk
½	teaspoon oregano
4	slices bacon, cooked and crumbled
½	cup sharp cheddar cheese, shredded
	Paprika

1.   Heat butter in an 8-inch omelet pan. Beat eggs with milk, stir in oregano. Pour egg mixture into pan and cook over medium-low heat until eggs begin to set. Sprinkle half the egg mixture with bacon and cheese; fold omelet in half. Heat thoroughly to melt cheese.

2.   Sprinkle with paprika; serve immediately.

Yield: 2 servings.

CHEESE DANISH

1½ packages active dry yeast
½ cup warm water
¾ cup milk, scalded and cooled to lukewarm
2 eggs, beaten
¼ cup granulated sugar
½ teaspoon salt
4 cups flour
1⅓ cups firm butter
⅓ cup flour
Beaten egg

Cheese Filling:
1 8-ounce package cream cheese
1 egg yolk
½ cup granulated sugar
½ teaspoon vanilla extract

Oven temperature: 450°

1. Soften yeast in ½ cup warm water in a large bowl.

2. Stir milk, eggs, sugar and salt into the yeast. Add 4 cups flour in fourths, beating until batter is smooth after each addition.

3. Using a pastry blender, cut butter into the ⅓ cup flour until mixture is well blended; set aside.

4. Turn dough onto a lightly floured surface; roll into a 14-inch square. Spread butter-flour mixture evenly over half the dough, leaving a 2-inch border.

5. Fold the dough in half and roll out to about ¼-inch thick. Fold in thirds and roll out; repeat this procedure three times. Wrap in plastic wrap and refrigerate for 30 minutes.

6. Meanwhile prepare Cheese Filling: Place cream cheese in small mixer bowl; beat until smooth and creamy. Add remaining ingredients and mix well.

7. Remove dough from refrigerator; working quickly on a lightly floured surface, roll dough into a 20-inch square.

8. Cut into 25 4-inch squares. Place a tablespoon of filling in the center of each square and bring corners in to center point.

9. Place on ungreased baking sheets and let rise in a warm place about 15 minutes. Brush tops with beaten egg.

10. Bake 6 to 10 minutes, until golden brown. Immediately remove from baking sheets to wire racks. Cool. Refrigerate or freeze.

11. Reheat 10–15 minutes in preheated oven before serving.

MENU • III

Friday Dinner
★ Faux Piccata Milanese ★
★ Parmesan Pasta ★
Whole Green Beans
★ Raspberry Roulade ★

Saturday Breakfast
Peaches and Cream
Soft Boiled Eggs
★ Toasted Whole Wheat Bread ★
Coffee

Saturday Lunch
★ Lemon Pasta ★
Assorted Cold Meats
Scallions
★ Almond Macaroons ★

Saturday Dinner
★ Grilled Lime Salmon Steaks ★
★ Florentine Rice ★
★ Glazed Carrots ★
Rolls
★ Chocolate Mint Icebox Cake ★

Sunday Brunch
Seedless Green Grapes
★ Mariners' Eggs ★
Toasted English Muffins
★ Blueberry Turnovers ★

FAUX PICCATA MILANESE

1 pork tenderloin
2 large eggs
1 tablespoon water
¾ cup bread crumbs
1 tablespoon chives, finely chopped
4 tablespoons butter
1 lemon, thinly sliced
  Parsley

1. Slice pork into 2-inch slices. Flatten each slice with a mallet between 2 sheets of waxed paper.

2. Beat eggs with water. Dip flattened slices of pork into egg mixture coating both sides. Dredge in bread crumbs mixed with chives to thoroughly coat. Refrigerate.

3. Melt butter in a skillet. Add pork tenderloin slices 2 or 3 at a time. Sauté until browned. Turn. Brown remaining side. Keep warm. Sauté remaining pork.

4. Serve garnished with lemon slices and parsley.

NOTE: Steps 1 and 2 may be completed at home to facilitate preparation onboard.

PARMESAN PASTA

1 pound fresh pasta
3 tablespoons butter
2 cloves garlic, minced
⅓ cup Parmesan cheese, grated
½ cup heavy cream
  Salt, freshly ground white pepper

1. Cook fresh pasta in boiling water for 1 to 2 minutes. Drain. Rinse in warm water. Reserve ⅓ to ½ for Lemon Pasta (Saturday lunch menu).

2. Melt butter in cooking pot. Add garlic; sauté for 2 to 3 minutes over medium heat. Add pasta, cheese, cream, and salt and pepper to taste. Heat thoroughly. Serve immediately.

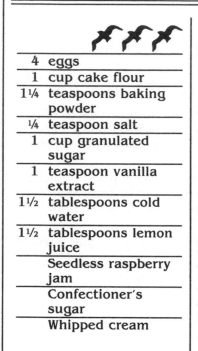

4	eggs
1	cup cake flour
1¼	teaspoons baking powder
¼	teaspoon salt
1	cup granulated sugar
1	teaspoon vanilla extract
1½	tablespoons cold water
1½	tablespoons lemon juice
	Seedless raspberry jam
	Confectioner's sugar
	Whipped cream

RASPBERRY ROULADE

Oven temperature: 350°

1. Separate eggs.

2. Sift flour, baking powder and salt. Set aside.

3. Beat egg whites with ¼ cup sugar until they hold soft peaks.

4. Without washing beaters, beat egg yolks until thick and lemon colored. Beat into yolk mixture vanilla, water, lemon juice and remaining ¾ cup sugar. Pour over whites and fold together until well blended. Fold in flour mixture. Pour into jelly roll pan, buttered and lined with buttered waxed paper. Bake 15 to 20 minutes or until done. Cake is done if it springs back when pressed lightly with finger.

5. Invert cake onto a clean dish towel, covered with sifted confectioner's sugar. Remove waxed paper. Roll up in towel until cool.

6. Unroll. Spread with raspberry jam. Roll up cake.

7. Serve slices with whipped cream.

½	cup warm water
1	package active dry yeast
1	cup milk
½	cup boiling water
¼	cup dark molasses
2	teaspoons salt
4	cups all-purpose flour
2	cups whole wheat flour

WHOLE WHEAT BREAD

Oven temperature: 375°

1. Add yeast to warm water.

2. In a separate bowl, mix milk, boiling water, molasses and salt. Cool to lukewarm. Add to yeast mixture. Stir in 3 cups flour. Beat thoroughly. Add remaining flour. Stir with a wooden spoon. Turn out onto floured surface; knead 5 minutes or until surface is smooth and not sticky. Let rise 1 hour or until doubled in bulk.

3. Shape into 2 loaves. Place in greased 7" x 5" bread pans and let rise again until doubled (1 hour).

4. Bake 50 minutes.

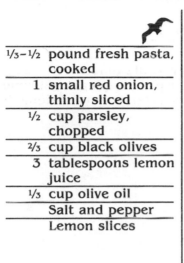

LEMON PASTA

1/3–1/2 pound fresh pasta, cooked
1 small red onion, thinly sliced
1/2 cup parsley, chopped
2/3 cup black olives
3 tablespoons lemon juice
1/3 cup olive oil
Salt and pepper
Lemon slices

1. Toss pasta together with onion, parsley and olives. Mix lemon juice and olive oil. Combine with pasta mixture. Salt and pepper to taste.

2. Garnish with lemon slices.

ALMOND MACAROONS

8 ounces almond paste
1 cup granulated sugar
3 egg whites
1/3 cup confectioner's sugar
2 tablespoons cake flour
1/8 teaspoon salt

Oven temperature: 300°

1. Mix almond paste in food processor. Gradually add sugar and egg whites. Blend thoroughly.

2. Place mixture in a bowl. Sift in sugar, flour and salt. Mix well.

3. Cover baking sheet with parchment or buttered waxed paper. Drop mixture by teaspoonsful on prepared baking sheet. Flatten with fingers dipped in cold water. Cover and let stand 2 hours or more.

4. Bake 30 minutes. Put parchment on a damp cloth and remove macaroons.

GRILLED LIME SALMON STEAKS

4 salmon steaks
1/4 cup lime juice
1/2 cup oil
1 teaspoon dried tarragon
Salt and pepper

1. Whisk lime juice together with oil. Add tarragon, salt and pepper.

2. Place salmon steaks in a shallow dish. Pour marinade over salmon. Refrigerate 4 hours or overnight.

3. Grill over hot coals until cooked to desired degree of doneness, approximately 5 minutes per side.

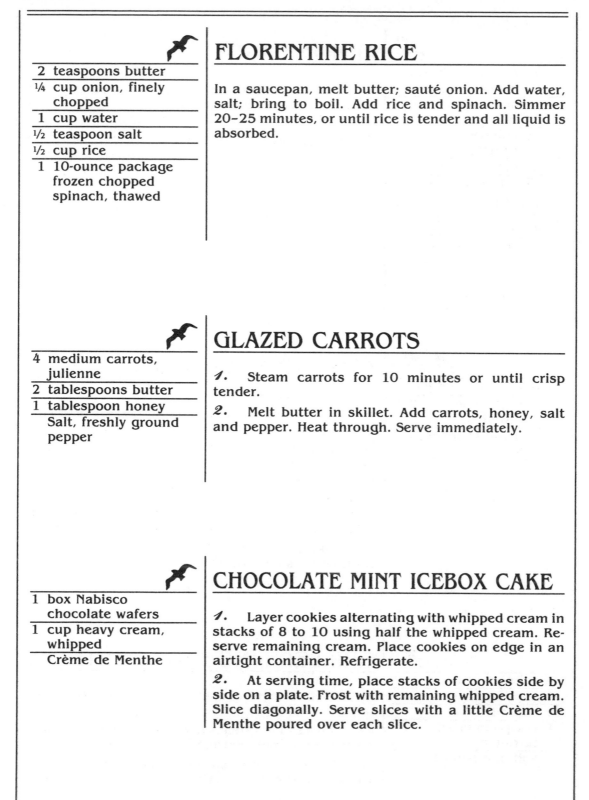

FLORENTINE RICE

2	teaspoons butter
¼	cup onion, finely chopped
1	cup water
½	teaspoon salt
½	cup rice
1	10-ounce package frozen chopped spinach, thawed

In a saucepan, melt butter; sauté onion. Add water, salt; bring to boil. Add rice and spinach. Simmer 20–25 minutes, or until rice is tender and all liquid is absorbed.

GLAZED CARROTS

4	medium carrots, julienne
2	tablespoons butter
1	tablespoon honey
	Salt, freshly ground pepper

1. Steam carrots for 10 minutes or until crisp tender.

2. Melt butter in skillet. Add carrots, honey, salt and pepper. Heat through. Serve immediately.

CHOCOLATE MINT ICEBOX CAKE

1	box Nabisco chocolate wafers
1	cup heavy cream, whipped
	Crème de Menthe

1. Layer cookies alternating with whipped cream in stacks of 8 to 10 using half the whipped cream. Reserve remaining cream. Place cookies on edge in an airtight container. Refrigerate.

2. At serving time, place stacks of cookies side by side on a plate. Frost with remaining whipped cream. Slice diagonally. Serve slices with a little Crème de Menthe poured over each slice.

MARINERS' EGGS

8 eggs
3 tablespoons milk
½ cup cottage cheese
3 tablespoons fresh
    chives, chopped
1 small tomato, peeled,
    seeded and chopped
3 tablespoons butter

1. Beat eggs with milk. Add cottage cheese, chives and tomato.

2. Melt butter in a skillet. Add egg mixture. Cook over medium heat stirring frequently until cooked, but still soft.

BLUEBERRY TURNOVERS

1 pint blueberries
¼ cup granulated
    sugar
3 tablespoons flour
Dash nutmeg
16 sheets phyllo dough
½ cup butter, melted
Bread crumbs

Oven temperature: 350°

1. Rinse blueberries. Drain well. Combine with sugar, flour and nutmeg. Set aside.

2. Keep phyllo covered with a damp towel to prevent it from drying out. Lay out 1 sheet of phyllo. Brush with butter and sprinkle with bread crumbs. Add a second layer of phyllo, butter and sprinkle with crumbs. Repeat until there are 8 sheets of phyllo stacked up. Form another stack, following the procedure for the remaining 8 sheets of phyllo. Cut both stacks in half, crosswise.

3. Across each stack of phyllo, draw an imaginary diagonal line. Place ¼ blueberry mixture on one side of the line on each of the stacks of phyllo. Fold in half diagonally. Crimp edges.

4. Place on baking sheet and bake for 35 minutes or until golden brown and bubbly.

5. May be reheated before serving.

Yield: 4 turnovers.

MENU · IV

Friday Dinner
★ Medallions of Beef with Madeira Sauce ★
Buttered Noodles
Fresh Asparagus
Rolls and Butter
★ Plum Clafouti ★

Saturday Breakfast
Fresh Orange Juice
Cold Cereal with Milk
★ Raspberry Kuchen ★
Coffee

Saturday Lunch
★ Tossed Salad with Lime Vinaigrette ★
French Bread and Butter
Vanilla Yogurt with Fresh Raspberries

Saturday Dinner
★ Chicken Stir Fry ★
Rice
★ Sourdough Rolls with Butter (see page 60) ★
★ Orange Compote ★

Sunday Brunch
★ Walnut and Cheese Omelet ★
★ Citrus Salad with Lemon Vinaigrette ★
★ Cinnamon Rolls ★
Coffee

MEDALLIONS OF BEEF WITH MADEIRA SAUCE

4	beef fillet steaks
2 tablespoons	butter
2 tablespoons	shallots, finely minced
1–1½ cups	brown sauce
2 tablespoons	lemon juice
¼ cup	Madeira wine

1. Melt butter in saucepan and sauté shallots for 5 minutes, taking care not to brown butter. Add brown sauce (available in jars in the specialty section of most supermarkets), and lemon juice. When liquid comes to a boil, add the wine and simmer gently for 5 minutes. Keep warm.

2. Grill fillets over hot coals to desired degree of doneness.

3. Serve immediately with Madeira Sauce.

PLUM CLAFOUTI

2 tablespoons	flour
¼ teaspoon	salt
1	egg
1 tablespoon	sour cream
⅓ cup	milk
1 teaspoon	lemon rind
1 teaspoon	butter
2 cups	purple plums, sliced

Oven temperature: 375°

1. Put flour, salt, egg, sour cream, milk and lemon rind in blender container and blend 1 minute on high speed.

2. Butter an ovenproof 8-inch skillet. Heat it on the stove. Pour ¼ batter in the pan and spread it over the entire bottom, as one would for a crêpe. Layer the fruit over the top of the batter. Pour remaining batter over the top. Bake 35 minutes.

3. The clafouti is best served heated.

4. Serve from a decorative plate. Cut in wedges.

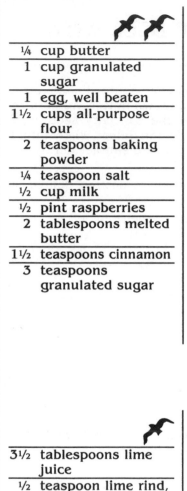

RASPBERRY KUCHEN

Oven temperature: 375°

¼	cup butter
1	cup granulated sugar
1	egg, well beaten
1½	cups all-purpose flour
2	teaspoons baking powder
¼	teaspoon salt
½	cup milk
½	pint raspberries
2	tablespoons melted butter
1½	teaspoons cinnamon
3	teaspoons granulated sugar

1. Cream butter. Beat in sugar and egg.

2. Sift together flour, baking powder, salt. Add to butter mixture alternately with milk. Mix well. Carefully fold in raspberries.

3. Place batter in a buttered 9-inch square pan. Sprinkle with melted butter, then a mixture of cinnamon and sugar. Bake about 20 minutes.

LIME VINAIGRETTE

3½	tablespoons lime juice
½	teaspoon lime rind, grated
1	teaspoon salt
½	teaspoon cracked black pepper
¾	cup olive oil

Combine all ingredients in a tightly covered jar. Shake well.

CHICKEN STIR FRY

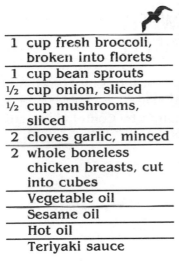

1 cup fresh broccoli, broken into florets
1 cup bean sprouts
½ cup onion, sliced
½ cup mushrooms, sliced
2 cloves garlic, minced
2 whole boneless chicken breasts, cut into cubes
Vegetable oil
Sesame oil
Hot oil
Teriyaki sauce

1. Heat 2 tablespoons vegetable oil and 1 teaspoon sesame oil in a large skillet or wok. Cook onion, broccoli and mushrooms over medium-high heat until mushrooms are browned. Remove to a heated plate. Add garlic and chicken. Add more oil, if necessary. Continue cooking until chicken is tender and juices run clear. Add bean sprouts. Cook 2 minutes. Add mushroom mixture. Heat through.

2. Sprinkle with hot oil and teriyaki sauce. Serve immediately with rice.

ORANGE COMPOTE

4 oranges, peeled and sectioned
½ cup flaked coconut
¼ cup Galliano
Fresh mint

Combine oranges with coconut. Divide equally among 4 serving dishes. Sprinkle each serving with 1 tablespoon Galliano. Serve garnished with fresh mint leaves.

WALNUT & CHEESE OMELET

8 eggs
4 tablespoons milk
4 tablespoons butter
4 tablespoons walnuts, chopped
4 tablespoons Bleu cheese, crumbled

1. Beat eggs with milk. Set aside.

2. Melt 1 tablespoon butter in omelet pan. Add ¼ egg mixture. Cook over medium heat, shaking pan to cook egg evenly. When cooked, add ¼ walnuts and ¼ cheese to center of omelet; fold edges over filling. Heat through. Serve immediately.

3. Repeat with remaining ingredients for 4 individual omelets.

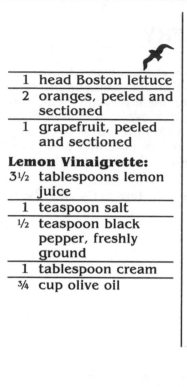

CITRUS SALAD WITH LEMON VINAIGRETTE

1 head Boston lettuce
2 oranges, peeled and sectioned
1 grapefruit, peeled and sectioned

Lemon Vinaigrette:
3½ tablespoons lemon juice
1 teaspoon salt
½ teaspoon black pepper, freshly ground
1 tablespoon cream
¾ cup olive oil

1. Rinse and dry lettuce. Tear into salad bowl. Add orange and grapefruit sections.

2. To prepare Lemon Vinaigrette: Combine ingredients in a jar. Shake well. Serve with Citrus Salad.

CINNAMON ROLLS

1 cup lukewarm water
1 package yeast
¼ cup granulated sugar
1 teaspoon salt
1½ teaspoons cinnamon
¼ cup soft butter
2 eggs
2½ cups flour
Melted butter
Confectioner's sugar
Vanilla extract

Oven temperature: 400°

1. In a large mixing bowl, add yeast to milk. Let stand 5 minutes. Stir. Add sugar, salt, cinnamon, butter and eggs. Beat thoroughly. Beat in 1½ cups flour. Let dough rise 40 minutes.

2. Mix in an additional 1 cup flour, more if necessary, to make dough firm enough to handle. Cover with plastic wrap. Chill ½ hour.

3. Knead dough 5 to 10 minutes or until smooth and not sticky. Roll and cut out as for biscuits. Arrange rolls in a 9-inch square pan, brush with melted butter. Cover with a clean towel. Let rise 1 hour or until doubled in size.

4. Bake about 20 minutes, or until delicately browned.

5. If desired, frost with confectioner's sugar moistened with water and flavored with vanilla.

MENU • V

Friday Dinner

★ Boursin Chicken Breasts ★
★ Brown Rice Pilaf ★
★ Cherry Tomatoes in Chive Cream ★
★ Strawberry Tarts ★

Saturday Breakfast

★ Fresh Tomato Juice ★
★ Scrambled Eggs en Croute ★
Coffee

Saturday Lunch

★ Chicken Rice Salad ★
★ Vegetarian Pockets ★
★ Raspberry Thumbprints ★

Saturday Dinner

★ Cajun Swordfish Grill ★
★ Barbecued Potatoes ★
★ Steamed Peppers and Mushrooms ★
★ Bananas Poached in White Wine
with Chocolate-Orange Sauce ★

Sunday Brunch

Orange Juice
★ Eggs Benedict Arnold ★
Fresh Raspberries in Chambord

BOURSIN CHICKEN BREASTS

4 whole chicken breasts, halved and pounded flat
8 ounces boursin cheese
2 eggs, slightly beaten Bread crumbs
4 tablespoons butter Lemon slices

1. Lay out flattened chicken breast halves. Spread each one with 1 ounce of boursin. Roll tightly. Secure with toothpicks, if necessary.

2. Dip chicken in beaten egg. Roll in crumbs. Refrigerate 1 hour before cooking. (May be done ahead to this stage.)

3. Melt butter in fry pan. Sauté chicken breasts until lightly browned and cooked through, about 3–4 minutes per side. Serve immediately, garnished with lemon slices.

NOTE: Use leftovers for chicken rice salad.

BROWN RICE PILAF

3 tablespoons butter
½ medium onion, chopped
½ medium red pepper, chopped
1 cup brown rice
1¾ cups chicken broth Freshly ground white pepper

Melt butter in a medium saucepan. Add onion and red pepper. Cook, stirring until onion is transparent, but not brown. Add rice and chicken broth. Bring mixture to a boil. Lower heat and simmer for 50–60 minutes, or until rice is tender and all liquid is absorbed. Add white pepper. Serve immediately.

NOTE: Use leftover rice for chicken rice salad.

CHERRY TOMATOES IN CHIVE CREAM

1 pint cherry tomatoes
2 tablespoons chives, chopped
¾ cup heavy cream Salt and freshly ground white pepper

In a fry pan, combine chives with heavy cream and cherry tomatoes. Cook over medium high heat until tomatoes are cooked and cream is reduced by half. Add salt and pepper to taste. Serve immediately.

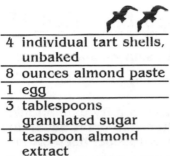

STRAWBERRY TARTS

4 individual tart shells, unbaked
8 ounces almond paste
1 egg
3 tablespoons granulated sugar
1 teaspoon almond extract
½ pint strawberries
½ cup apricot jam, strained

Oven temperature: 400°

1. Combine almond paste, egg, sugar and almond extract in food processor with metal blade.

2. Divide almond mixture equally among tart shells. Bake in a preheated oven for 15 minutes or until tart shells are lightly browned. Cool.

3. Wash, hull and halve strawberries. Arrange strawberries over tarts. Brush with apricot jam. Refrigerate.

FRESH TOMATO JUICE

10–12 tomatoes, sliced
¼ cup vinegar
1 teaspoon granulated sugar
1 teaspoon salt
1 bay leaf
¼ cup celery leaves, chopped
¼ cup onion, chopped
4 celery stalks to garnish

1. Combine all ingredients in a pan. Bring to boil. Simmer 30 minutes.

2. Strain. Chill in refrigerator until serving. Garnish with a stalk of celery.

SCRAMBLED EGGS EN CROUTE

8 eggs
¼ cup sour cream
6 tablespoons butter
8 slices of bread
1 teaspoon orange rind, grated
1 orange

1. Beat eggs together with sour cream. Set aside.

2. With a 3-inch round biscuit cutter, cut circles from bread slices.

3. Melt 4 tablespoons butter in a fry pan. Sprinkle grated orange rind over butter. Add bread slices and lightly brown on both sides. Set aside. Keep warm.

4. Melt 2 tablespoons butter in a fry pan (the same one is fine). Add egg and sour cream mixture. Cook, stirring, to desired degree of doneness.

5. Serve eggs immediately over bread rounds. Garnish with fresh orange slices.

CHICKEN RICE SALAD

1 cup rice, cooked
2 tablespoons oil
¾ cup chicken meat, cooked and chopped coarsely
¾ cup seedless grapes, halved
3 tablespoons onion, minced
1 teaspoon dried tarragon
1 tablespoon fresh parsley, finely chopped
Salt and pepper
⅓ cup mayonnaise

Mix oil with cooked rice. Add chicken, grapes, onion, tarragon, parsley, salt and pepper. Toss. Combine with mayonnaise. Serve chilled.

VEGETARIAN POCKETS

4 small pitas
4 large mushrooms, sliced
1 red pepper, julienne
16 snow peas
4 artichoke hearts, sliced
Lettuce
Vinaigrette dressing (see recipe)
Salt and pepper

Split pitas to create "pockets." Stuff with equal amounts of mushrooms, red pepper, snow peas, artichokes, and lettuce. Sprinkle with Lemon or Lime Vinaigrette. Add salt and pepper to taste.

RASPBERRY THUMBPRINTS

¼ cup brown sugar
½ cup butter
1 egg, separated
½ teaspoon vanilla extract
1 cup flour
¼ teaspoon salt
¾ cup walnuts, finely chopped
1 cup seedless raspberry jam

Oven temperature: 350°

1. Mix brown sugar, butter, egg yolk and vanilla. Mix in flour and salt. Shape dough into 1-inch balls.

2. Beat egg white slightly. Dip each ball in egg white; roll in nuts. Place balls 1-inch apart on ungreased baking sheet. Press thumbs deeply in the center of each. Bake 10 minutes or until lightly browned.

3. Remove from baking sheet immediately; cool. Fill thumbprints with raspberry jam.

CAJUN SWORDFISH GRILL

4 swordfish steaks
3 shallots, minced
1 cup milk
1 teaspoon salt
2 tablespoons Tabasco
1 teaspoon thyme
1 teaspoon oregano
1 teaspoon cayenne
   pepper

1.   Combine milk with shallots, salt, Tabasco, thyme, oregano and cayenne pepper. Add swordfish steaks and marinate at least 1 hour.

2.   Grill swordfish over very hot coals until browned on the outside and just done on the inside, 3–5 minutes per side. Brush frequently with marinade. Do not overcook.

BARBECUED POTATOES

4 medium baking
   potatoes
6 tablespoons butter,
   melted
1 envelope dry onion
   soup mix

A covered barbecue grill works best.

Wash potatoes, slice in ¼-inch slices about ¾ of the way through the potato. Spread slices apart and sprinkle with onion soup mix. Drizzle potatoes with melted butter. Wrap in foil and place on hot coals 45 minutes to 1 hour or until tender.

NOTE: There are a couple of "do ahead" options for this recipe.
   1.   After raw potatoes are wrapped in foil, they may be kept in the refrigerator or icebox until cooking time.
   2.   Potatoes may be baked at home at 400° for 1 hour, refrigerated, and reheated at serving time. Do not try to keep them more than a day, however.

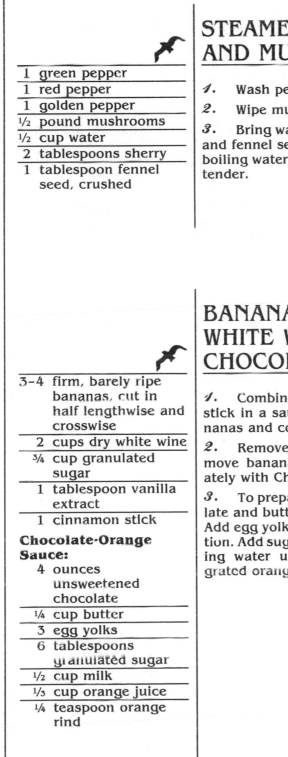

STEAMED PEPPERS AND MUSHROOMS

1	green pepper
1	red pepper
1	golden pepper
½	pound mushrooms
½	cup water
2	tablespoons sherry
1	tablespoon fennel seed, crushed

1. Wash peppers, remove seeds and julienne.

2. Wipe mushrooms and slice.

3. Bring water and sherry to a boil. Add vegetables and fennel seeds to steamer basket and place above boiling water. Steam for 5–7 minutes or until "crisp" tender.

BANANAS POACHED IN WHITE WINE WITH CHOCOLATE-ORANGE SAUCE

3–4	firm, barely ripe bananas, cut in half lengthwise and crosswise
2	cups dry white wine
¾	cup granulated sugar
1	tablespoon vanilla extract
1	cinnamon stick

Chocolate-Orange Sauce:

4	ounces unsweetened chocolate
¼	cup butter
3	egg yolks
6	tablespoons granulated sugar
½	cup milk
⅓	cup orange juice
¼	teaspoon orange rind

1. Combine wine, sugar, vanilla and cinnamon stick in a saucepan. Simmer for 5 minutes. Add bananas and cook 5 minutes at just below simmer.

2. Remove from heat and let stand 20 minutes. Remove bananas from cooking liquid. Serve immediately with Chocolate-Orange Sauce.

3. To prepare Chocolate-Orange Sauce: Melt chocolate and butter in a double boiler. Stir until blended. Add egg yolks one at a time, beating after each addition. Add sugar and milk. Cook, stirring, over simmering water until thickened. Add orange juice and grated orange rind. Blend thoroughly. Serve warm.

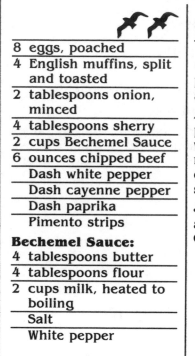

EGGS BENEDICT ARNOLD

8 eggs, poached

4 English muffins, split and toasted

2 tablespoons onion, minced

4 tablespoons sherry

2 cups Bechemel Sauce

6 ounces chipped beef

  Dash white pepper

  Dash cayenne pepper

  Dash paprika

  Pimento strips

Bechemel Sauce:

4 tablespoons butter

4 tablespoons flour

2 cups milk, heated to boiling

  Salt

  White pepper

1. Combine onion, sherry, chipped beef, white pepper, cayenne, and paprika with Bechemel Sauce. Set aside. Keep warm.

2. To prepare Bechemel Sauce: In a medium saucepan, melt butter. Add flour and cook, stirring with a wire whisk, over low heat for 3–5 minutes, or until mixture is golden, but not browned. Add milk all at once. Cook stirring constantly until thickened. Add salt and pepper to taste.

3. Butter English muffin halves. Top each half with a poached egg. Pour white sauce mixture over all. Garnish with pimento strips.

5

AN ELEGANT
WEEKEND

Do not, I repeat, do not be intimidated by this chapter. If you enjoy eating good food and feeling pampered, you will wonder why you never cooked this way before, and what all the fuss was about, anyway.

There has always been a mystique surrounding gourmet cooking. Let's clear away some of that—at least enough so that you understand that you needn't be Julia Child to prepare a sumptuous meal.

If, per chance, you glanced at the menus and saw Eggs Benedict, you may be saying to yourself, "Who does she think she's kidding; I've never made that at home, never mind on a two-burner alcohol stove." Take heart! Each menu item will be broken into its basic components and I will lead you, one step at a time, through the meal preparation. The most difficult element you must face in the preparation of Eggs Benedict is poaching eggs. If you can boil water and if you have a timer, there is no reason they won't be perfect.

Again, you may be thinking, "But hollandaise . . . me? It'll never happen . . ." That's a place where you have some options. My first choice, admittedly the most difficult, is preparing the hollandaise on the boat in conjunction with the rest of the meal. If that's more than you choose to manage, I have included a wonderful recipe for blender hollandaise which can be prepared at home, transported and reheated successfully. Beyond that, you may choose from mock hollandaise, packaged mixes to which you add a couple of simple ingredients, or prepared hollandaise in a jar. Select the finest brands when you purchase prepared hollandaise sauce or a mix; and you must be aware that the quality of the finished product will suffer to some degree. But you know best what will suit your needs, your goals, your mood, and your energy level.

Be daring. This is an adventure and like any adventure there will be challenges and rewards. The rewards will depend upon the earnestness of your efforts, and I believe you will find them truly worthwhile. As in any endeavor, the more you practice, the easier it becomes.

And with that, let's begin preparation for an elegant weekend of sun, sailing and dining.

MENU ◆ I

Friday Dinner

★ Gazpacho ★

★ Grilled Lamb Chops with Rosemary Mint Sauce ★

Steamed New Potatoes with Dill

Buttered Peas

★ Herb Bread/Butter ★

★ Banana Sauté with Grand Marnier ★

Saturday Breakfast

Cantaloupe with Lime

★ Mexican Omelet ★

★ Almond Croissants ★

★ Brioche ★

Jam/Marmalade

Coffee/Tea

Saturday Lunch

★ Langoustino Salad with Avocado ★

★ Deviled Eggs ★

★ French Bread/Butter ★

★ Chocolate Chunk Cookies ★

Saturday Dinner

★ Artichokes with Crabmeat Sauce ★

★ Cornish Game Hens with Raspberry Glaze ★

★ Curried Orange Rice ★

Steamed Broccoli with Lemon Butter

★ Bib Lettuce with Garlic Vinaigrette ★

French Rolls/Butter

★ Chocolate Mousse ★

★ Shortbread ★

Sunday Brunch

★ Mimosas ★

Strawberries and Kiwi

★ Eggs Benedict ★

Coffee/Tea

GAZPACHO

1 clove garlic
4 ripe tomatoes, quartered
½ green pepper, seeded and sliced
½ small onion, peeled and sliced
1 cucumber, peeled and coarsely sliced
1 teaspoon salt
¼ teaspoon pepper
2 teaspoons chili powder
2 tablespoons olive oil
3 tablespoons red wine vinegar
½ cup ice water
Chopped vegetables to garnish

1. Add all ingredients to blender or food processor container. Cover and blend on high speed for 3–5 seconds, or until vegetables are coarsely chopped.

2. Chill. Serve garnished with chopped vegetables.

GRILLED LAMB CHOPS WITH ROSEMARY MINT SAUCE

8 loin lamb chops
⅓ cup apple mint jelly
1–1½ teaspoons dried rosemary

1. Melt mint jelly with rosemary. Brush mixture on lamb chops.

2. Grill chops to desired degree of doneness, brushing often with sauce.

HERB BREAD

Oven temperature: 400°

1. Soften yeast in warm water.

2. Blend milk, butter, sugar and salt thoroughly in a large separate bowl; cool to warm. Add 1 cup flour and beat well. Beat in egg, nutmeg and sage, then yeast. Mix in enough remaining flour to make a soft (not sticky) dough.

3. Turn onto a lightly floured surface and knead 5 to 10 minutes or until smooth and elastic. Put into a greased deep bowl; turn dough so greased surface is on top. Cover; let rise in a warm place until doubled, about 1 hour.

4. Punch down dough and let rest 10 minutes.

5. Shape dough into a round loaf. Place in a greased 9-inch pie pan and let rise again until doubled, 45 minutes to 1 hour.

6. Preheat oven to 400°. Brush lightly with slightly beaten egg white. Sprinkle with caraway seeds.

7. Bake for 10 minutes; reduce oven temperature to 375° and bake 20–25 minutes or until well browned.

1	package active dry yeast
¼	cup warm water
¾	cup milk, scalded
3	tablespoons butter
3	tablespoons granulated sugar
1½	teaspoons salt
3–3½	cups all-purpose flour
1	egg, beaten
¼	teaspoon ground nutmeg
3	teaspoons sage
	Egg white, slightly beaten
	Caraway seeds

BANANA SAUTÉ WITH GRAND MARNIER

4	bananas
5	tablespoons butter
¼	cup Grand Marnier
½	teaspoon cinnamon

1. Peel bananas. Cut in half lengthwise and crosswise.

2. Heat butter in sauté pan. Add bananas and sauté until slightly brown, but not soft, about 1 minute per side.

3. Add Grand Marnier to pan and flame. (Be careful to flame away from curtains and other flammable materials.)

4. Serve on individual plates. Sprinkle with cinnamon.

MEXICAN OMELET

2 tablespoons butter
4 eggs
2 tablespoons milk
½ ripe avocado, chopped
½ medium tomato, seeded and chopped
12 ripe olives, sliced
½ cup jalepeno pepper cheese, shredded
Chopped tomato
Sour cream

1. Melt butter in 10-inch omelet pan. Beat eggs with milk; add to pan. Cook over medium-low heat until eggs begin to set. Sprinkle half the egg mixture with avocado, tomato, olives and cheese. Fold in half. Heat through to melt cheese.

2. Serve immediately garnished with chopped tomato and sour cream.

Serves 2.

BRIOCHE

½ cup butter
⅓ cup granulated sugar
½ teaspoon salt
½ cup heavy cream
1 package active dry yeast
¼ cup warm water
1 egg yolk
2 eggs
3¼ cups all-purpose flour
1 egg white, unbeaten
1 tablespoon granulated sugar

Oven temperature: 375°

1. Cream butter with ⅓ cup sugar and salt in a large bowl. Beat in cream.

2. Soften yeast in warm water.

3. In a separate bowl, beat egg yolk with 2 eggs until thick. Gradually add to the creamed mixture, beating constantly until fluffy. Blend in yeast.

4. Add flour ½ cup at a time, beating thoroughly after each addition. Cover; let rise in a warm place until doubled, about 2 hours.

5. Stir down and beat thoroughly. Cover tightly with plastic wrap and refrigerate overnight.

6. Remove from refrigerator and stir down the dough. Turn onto a lightly floured surface and divide into 2 portions, one about ¾ of the dough, the other ¼.

7. Cut each portion into 16 equal pieces. Roll each piece into a smooth ball. Place each large ball in a well-greased muffin tin well. Make a deep indentation with finger in the center of each large ball; moisten each depression slightly with cold water. Press a small ball into each depression.

8. Cover; let rise again until more than doubled, about 1 hour.

9. Preheat oven to 375°. Brush tops of rolls with a mixture of egg white and 1 tablespoon sugar.

10. Bake 15 minutes or until golden brown.

NOTE: See recipe for Cheese Danish pastry

follow steps 1–7.

Almond Filling:
8 ounces almond paste
¼ cup granulated sugar
1 egg, slightly beaten
½ teaspoon almond extract

ALMOND CROISSANTS

Oven temperature: 450°

8. To prepare Almond Filling: Combine all ingredients in blender or food processor until well combined and of spreading consistency. Set aside.

9. Cut dough lengthwise into 4 equal strips. Cut each strip into 7 triangles. Spread triangles with Almond Filling and roll up toward point of the triangle.

10. Place on ungreased baking sheets and let rise in a warm place about 15 minutes. Brush tops with beaten eggs.

11. Bake 6–10 minutes, until golden brown. Immediately remove from baking sheets to wire racks.

12. Reheat in a preheated 325° oven before serving.

8	ounces langoustino, thawed
1	tablespoon chives
1½	teaspoons tarragon, minced
2	tablespoons onion, finely chopped
½	teaspoon paprika
½	teaspoon Dijon-style mustard
¼	cup mayonnaise
1	teaspoon sherry
1	avocado, sliced
	Lettuce
	Lemon

LANGOUSTINO SALAD

1. Combine first 4 ingredients and set aside.

2. Mix remaining ingredients together in a small bowl until thoroughly blended. Add to langoustino mixture and toss until well coated. Chill.

3. Arrange avocado slices on a bed of lettuce on four plates. Mound langoustino salad on lettuce alongside avocado slices. Garnish each serving with a lemon slice.

NOTE: Langouste are spring lobsters from Europe. They have a more delicate flavor than most lobster varieties.

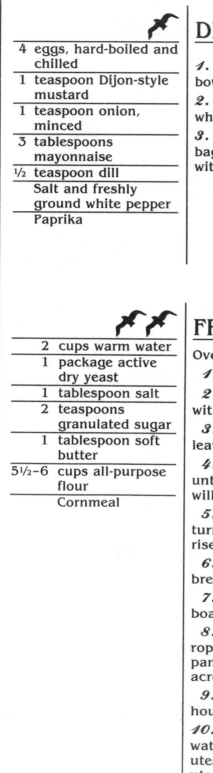

DEVILED EGGS

4 eggs, hard-boiled and chilled
1 teaspoon Dijon-style mustard
1 teaspoon onion, minced
3 tablespoons mayonnaise
½ teaspoon dill
Salt and freshly ground white pepper
Paprika

1. Peel eggs. Cut in half, lengthwise. Put yolks in bowl. Reserve whites.

2. Mash yolks. Add mustard, onion, dill, salt and white pepper. Combine with mayonnaise.

3. Return yolk mixture to egg whites with a pastry bag fitted with a star tip, or with a spoon. Sprinkle with paprika. Chill.

FRENCH BREAD

2 cups warm water
1 package active dry yeast
1 tablespoon salt
2 teaspoons granulated sugar
1 tablespoon soft butter
5½–6 cups all-purpose flour
Cornmeal

Oven temperature: 300°

1. Dissolve yeast in warm water in a large bowl.

2. Add salt, sugar, butter and 2 cups flour; beat with a wooden spoon until smooth.

3. Gradually add remaining flour, until dough leaves sides of bowl.

4. Turn dough onto a lightly floured board. Knead until smooth and elastic—about 10 minutes. Dough will be stiff.

5. Place dough in a lightly greased, large bowl; turn so greased side is up. Cover with a towel and let rise until doubled—about 1½ hours.

6. Lightly grease a large baking sheet or French bread pans and sprinkle with cornmeal.

7. Punch down dough; turn onto lightly floured board. Divide in thirds.

8. With hands, roll each third into a 14-inch long rope. Place 3 inches apart on baking sheet or in bread pans. Brush with cold water; cut 4 diagonal slashes across each loaf.

9. Let rise uncovered until doubled—about 1½ hours.

10. Preheat oven to 300°. Place shallow pan of water on bottom of oven. Bake loaves 40 to 50 minutes, spraying or brushing with water every 20 minutes. Remove loaves to wire rack and cool.

CHOCOLATE CHUNK COOKIES

Oven temperature: 350°

½ cup unsalted butter, at room temperature
½ cup dark brown sugar, firmly packed
½ cup granulated sugar
1 teaspoon vanilla extract
½ teaspoon salt
1 egg
½ teaspoon baking soda
¾ cup flour
1 cup rolled oats
½ cup Heath Bar brickel
12 ounces bittersweet chocolate, coarsely chopped

1. In a large mixing bowl, combine the butter, brown sugar, sugar, vanilla and salt. Beat with a spoon until fluffy. Beat in the egg, baking soda and 1 teaspoon water. Stir in the flour, oats, brickel and chocolate. Transfer to a bowl just large enough to hold the dough, cover and refrigerate for 1–2 hours.

2. Preheat oven to 350°. Lightly coat baking sheet with vegetable shortening. Use 2–3 tablespoons dough for each cookie. Shape the dough into balls and place one in the center of the baking sheet and evenly space 4 others a few inches in from each corner. Bake for 10–12 minutes. Do not overbake.

3. Cool on sheet for 2 minutes. Transfer to paper towels for about 2 minutes and transfer to racks to cool.

ARTICHOKES WITH CRABMEAT SAUCE

4 whole artichokes
1 tablespoon lemon juice
1 teaspoon salt
1 teaspoon tarragon

Crabmeat Sauce:
⅓ cup mayonnaise
1 tablespoon Dijon-style mustard
½ teaspoon Worcestershire sauce
1 tablespoon green onion, minced
4 ounces flaked crabmeat

1. Wash and trim artichoke stems and leaves.

2. Cook artichokes in 2 inches of boiling water with lemon juice, salt and tarragon. Cook for 45 minutes to 1 hour, or until leaves pull away easily.

3. Drain, remove choke from center and serve immediately on individual plates with Crabmeat Sauce in the center of artichokes.

4. To prepare Crabmeat Sauce, mix all ingredients together until well combined.

CORNISH GAME HENS WITH RASPBERRY GLAZE

2	large Cornish game hens, halved
1/3	cup seedless raspberry jam
1/4	cup Grand Marnier
1	teaspoon grated orange rind
	Fresh raspberries

1. Wash hens and pat dry.

2. Combine remaining ingredients except fresh berries, and mix well.

3. Brush Cornish hens with glaze. Grill over hot coals 35–45 minutes or until tender, brushing frequently with glaze. Serve immediately with fresh raspberries.

CURRIED ORANGE RICE

3	tablespoons butter
1	medium onion, thinly sliced
1 1/2	teaspoons curry powder
3/4	cup uncooked rice
3/4	cup orange juice
3/4	cup chicken broth
1/2	teaspoon salt
1/3	cup seedless raisins

1. Melt butter in a saucepan or flame-proof casserole; sauté onion until soft and golden, but not browned. Stir in curry and rice; cook 2 minutes, stirring constantly.

2. Add remaining ingredients; stir. Bring to boiling; lower heat; cover; simmer 20–25 minutes or until rice is tender and liquid has been absorbed.

GARLIC VINAIGRETTE

2	cloves garlic, minced
1/2	teaspoon salt
2	tablespoons lemon juice
1/2	cup extra virgin olive oil
1/2	teaspoon basil
	White pepper, freshly ground

1. Combine garlic, salt; beat in lemon juice and olive oil; add basil and white pepper.

2. Shake well before serving.

CHOCOLATE MOUSSE

6	ounces semisweet chocolate bits
2	whole eggs
3	tablespoons strong hot coffee
2	teaspoons rum
¾	cup milk, scalded

1. Put all ingredients in blender container. Blend on high speed for 2 minutes.

2. Pour into 4 small containers that can be tightly covered. Chill in refrigerator for 4 hours or overnight.

3. Serve garnished with whipped cream and shaved chocolate.

NOTE: This recipe may be prepared up to 3 days before serving. It keeps very well in an icebox as long as it is on the ice.

SHORTBREAD

1	pound butter
1	cup granulated sugar
5	cups sifted flour
1	teaspoon salt

Oven temperature: 350°

1. Soften butter; add sugar and beat until light and fluffy.

2. Add flour. Mix with pastry blender until thoroughly combined. Do not use spoon or electric mixer.

3. Press mixture into 2 greased 8-inch square pans. Prick the top of the dough with a fork.

4. Bake 35–40 minutes or until golden and firm to the touch.

5. Cut into squares while still warm. Allow to cool before removing from pan.

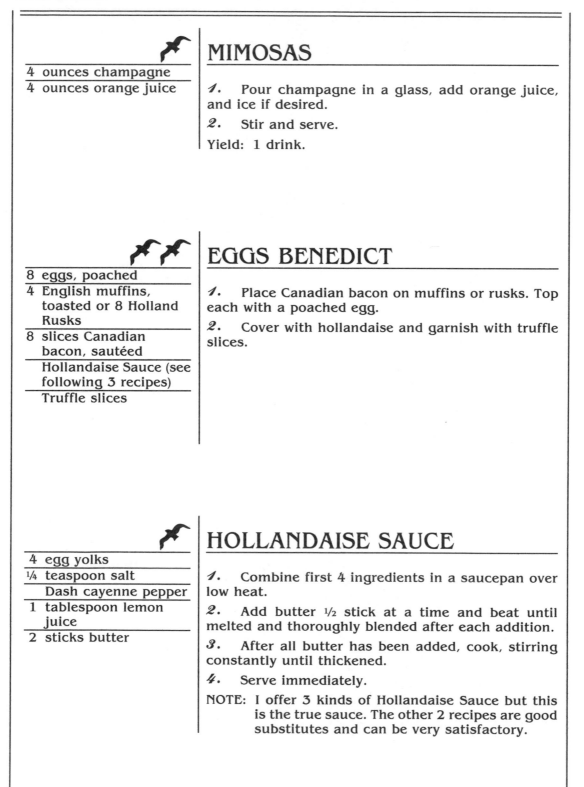

MIMOSAS

4 ounces champagne
4 ounces orange juice

1. Pour champagne in a glass, add orange juice, and ice if desired.

2. Stir and serve.

Yield: 1 drink.

EGGS BENEDICT

8 eggs, poached
4 English muffins, toasted or 8 Holland Rusks
8 slices Canadian bacon, sautéed
Hollandaise Sauce (see following 3 recipes)
Truffle slices

1. Place Canadian bacon on muffins or rusks. Top each with a poached egg.

2. Cover with hollandaise and garnish with truffle slices.

HOLLANDAISE SAUCE

4 egg yolks
¼ teaspoon salt
Dash cayenne pepper
1 tablespoon lemon juice
2 sticks butter

1. Combine first 4 ingredients in a saucepan over low heat.

2. Add butter ½ stick at a time and beat until melted and thoroughly blended after each addition.

3. After all butter has been added, cook, stirring constantly until thickened.

4. Serve immediately.

NOTE: I offer 3 kinds of Hollandaise Sauce but this is the true sauce. The other 2 recipes are good substitutes and can be very satisfactory.

BLENDER HOLLANDAISE SAUCE

4 egg yolks
¼ teaspoon salt
Dash cayenne pepper
1 tablespoon lemon juice
1 cup butter, melted

1.   Place egg yolks, salt, cayenne pepper, and lemon juice in blender container. Blend 30–45 seconds.

2.   Remove center portion of blender container cover and replace with a funnel.

3.   With blender on low speed, pour melted butter *slowly* through funnel, until all has been added and sauce is well mixed.

NOTE: May be refrigerated and reheated at a later time *carefully* over low heat or in the top of a double boiler.

MOCK HOLLANDAISE

2 tablespoons butter
2 tablespoons flour
1 cup milk
Salt and pepper
2 egg yolks
6 tablespoons butter
1 tablespoon lemon juice

1.   In a medium saucepan, melt 2 tablespoons butter. Add flour. Stir with a wire whisk. Cook, stirring constantly, until flour is golden, but not browned.

2.   Add milk. Stir constantly until thickened and smooth.*

3.   Just before serving, reheat, stir in egg yolks, 6 tablespoons butter, 1 tablespoon at a time, and lemon juice.

*May be cooled at this point and stored, refrigerated, in a covered container.

MENU • II

Friday Dinner

★ Curried Eggs ★
★ Scallop Kabobs ★
★ Saffron Rice ★
★ Belgian Endive with Walnut Dressing ★
★ Egg Twist Bread/Butter ★
★ Strawberry-Almond Crêpes ★

Saturday Breakfast

Peaches and Cream
★ Blueberry Muffins/Butter ★
★ Ham Omelet with Cheese Sauce ★
Coffee

Saturday Lunch

★ Creamy Cucumber Soup ★
★ Chicken with Almonds ★
★ Marinated Mushrooms & Artichoke Hearts ★
Black Bread/Butter
★ Chocolate-Orange Truffles ★

Saturday Dinner

★ Mussels in Snail Butter ★
★ Cold Poached Salmon with Sauce Remoulade ★
★ Pasta Artichoke Salad ★
★ Sautéed Vegetables ★
French Bread/Butter
★ Blueberries with Lemon Cream ★

Sunday Brunch

★ Bloody Mary ★
Fresh Fruit Compote
★ Eggs Adrienne ★
Coffee/Tea

CURRIED EGGS

4 eggs, hard-boiled and chilled

2 tablespoons chutney

¼ teaspoon salt

Dash white pepper, freshly ground

½ cup mayonnaise (see recipe)

1 teaspoon curry powder

½ teaspoon Worcestershire sauce

3 tablespoons heavy cream

Parsley

1. Trim a thin slice off the bottom of each hard-boiled egg. Cut the eggs in half, lengthwise.

2. Place yolks in a small bowl, mash. Add chutney, salt and pepper. Mix well.

3. Stuff egg whites with yolk mixture. Place 2 halves of egg together and stand on end. Chill.

4. Meanwhile blend mayonnaise with curry powder, Worcestershire sauce, and cream.

5. To serve stand eggs on individual plates. Spoon sauce over top. Garnish with fresh parsley.

SCALLOP KABOBS

1 pound scallops

1 red pepper, cut in chunks

16 mushrooms

1 medium onion, quartered

16 cherry tomatoes

1 medium summer squash, thickly sliced

Garlic vinaigrette (see recipe) or use your favorite bottled vinaigrette with the addition of some minced garlic

1. Arrange all ingredients alternately on 8 skewers. Brush with vinaigrette.

2. Grill about 10–12 minutes over hot coals, basting frequently with vinaigrette and turning.

WALNUT DRESSING

3 tablespoons lemon juice
1/4 cup vegetable oil
1/4 cup walnut oil
1/4 teaspoon salt
1/4 cup walnuts, finely chopped

Combine all ingredients. Shake well.

EGG TWIST BREAD

2 cups milk
3 tablespoons granulated sugar
1 tablespoon salt
1/4 cup butter
1/4 cup warm water
2 packages active dry yeast
2 eggs, slightly beaten
7 1/4 cups all-purpose flour, sifted
Beaten egg yolk

Oven temperature: 400°

1. Heat milk until bubbles just form around the edge. Remove from heat. Add sugar, salt, 1/4 cup butter, stirring until butter is melted. Let cool to lukewarm.

2. Sprinkle yeast over water in a large bowl, stirring until dissolved. Stir in milk mixture. Add eggs.

3. Add half the flour; beat with a wooden spoon until smooth—about 2 minutes. Gradually add remaining flour, mixing with hands until dough is stiff enough to leave sides of bowl.

4. Turn out dough onto lightly floured board. Cover with the bowl; let rest 10 minutes. Knead 10 minutes or until dough is smooth and elastic.

5. Place in lightly greased bowl; turn to bring greased side up. Cover with towel; let rise about 1 hour or until double in bulk.

6. Punch dough down and turn out on lightly floured board.

7. To shape into 2 braids: divide dough in half. Cut each half into 6 equal parts. Roll each part into a 12-inch strip.

8. Braid 3 strips together; place on greased baking sheet. Braid 3 more strips. Place directly on top of first braid. Press ends together to seal. Repeat with remaining 6 strips of dough, making a second braided loaf.

9. Cover with towel; let rise until doubled—about 1 hour. Preheat oven to 400°. Brush with beaten egg yolk mixed with 1 tablespoon water.

10. Bake braids 40 minutes or until braids are a deep golden brown. Remove to wire racks. Cool completely.

SAFFRON RICE

½	medium onion, chopped
½	teaspoon saffron
2	tablespoons butter
¾	cup rice
1½	cups chicken broth

1. Melt butter in saucepan. Add onion and saffron. Cook until onion is soft and golden, but not brown.

2. Add rice and cook for 2 minutes. Add chicken broth; bring to boiling. Lower heat and simmer for 25–30 minutes or until rice is tender and all liquid is absorbed.

STRAWBERRY-ALMOND CRÊPES

1	cup all-purpose flour, sifted
3	eggs
¾	cup milk
¾	cup water
¼	teaspoon salt
2	tablespoons butter, melted

Strawberry-Almond Filling:

2	cups sour cream
3	tablespoons granulated sugar
2	tablespoons Amaretto
2	cups strawberries, sliced and sweetened
2	tablespoons butter
	Confectioner's sugar

1. Place crêpe ingredients in blender container in order given. Blend 30 seconds, stop and stir down sides. Blend 30 to 60 seconds, or until smooth.

2. Cook according to crêpe maker directions or in an 8-inch crêpe pan over medium-high heat. Melt 1 teaspoon butter; add 2 tablespoons batter. Swirl batter around pan as crêpe cooks so it will be very thin. When top is dry, turn crêpe; quickly cook second side.

3. Remove from pan. Repeat until all batter is used. Cool. Crêpes may be frozen at this point or used immediately.

4. To prepare filling: Combine sour cream, sugar and Amaretto. Spread crêpes with an equal amount of sour cream mixture and a few sliced berries, reserving some berries for garnish; roll up.

5. Arrange rolls in shallow casserole; cover and store in refrigerator until serving time.

6. To heat, melt butter in a sauté pan over medium-low heat. Heat crêpes, turning carefully to heat evenly. Add remaining strawberries, heat. Sprinkle with confectioner's sugar.

NOTE: Crêpes may also be served at room temperature.

Yield: 16 crêpes.

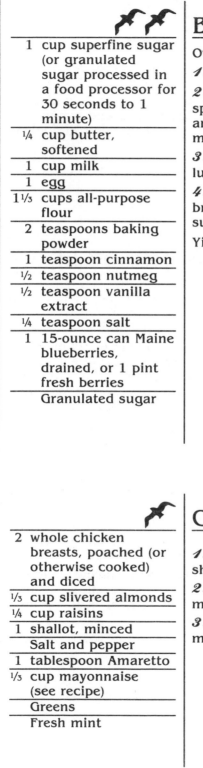

BLUEBERRY MUFFINS

Oven temperature: 375°

1. Prepare muffin tin with paper liners.

2. In medium bowl, cream sugar and butter on low speed of electric mixer until smooth. Add milk, egg, and half the flour, baking powder, cinnamon, nutmeg, vanilla and salt; mix until just blended.

3. Gently mix in remaining flour (batter will be lumpy). Fold in blueberries.

4. Fill muffin tin liners ¾ full. Bake until golden brown, 20–30 minutes. Sprinkle with granulated sugar. Serve warm.

Yield: 12 muffins.

Ingredients (Blueberry Muffins):

- 1 cup superfine sugar (or granulated sugar processed in a food processor for 30 seconds to 1 minute)
- ¼ cup butter, softened
- 1 cup milk
- 1 egg
- 1⅓ cups all-purpose flour
- 2 teaspoons baking powder
- 1 teaspoon cinnamon
- ½ teaspoon nutmeg
- ½ teaspoon vanilla extract
- ¼ teaspoon salt
- 1 15-ounce can Maine blueberries, drained, or 1 pint fresh berries
- Granulated sugar

CHICKEN WITH ALMONDS

1. Combine chicken breasts, almonds, raisins and shallot. Add salt and pepper to taste.

2. Stir Amaretto into mayonnaise. Add to chicken mixture. Stir gently to thoroughly combine. Chill.

3. Serve on a bed of greens, garnished with fresh mint.

Ingredients (Chicken with Almonds):

- 2 whole chicken breasts, poached (or otherwise cooked) and diced
- ⅓ cup slivered almonds
- ¼ cup raisins
- 1 shallot, minced
- Salt and pepper
- 1 tablespoon Amaretto
- ⅓ cup mayonnaise (see recipe)
- Greens
- Fresh mint

HAM OMELET WITH CHEESE SAUCE

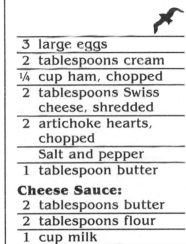

3 large eggs
2 tablespoons cream
¼ cup ham, chopped
2 tablespoons Swiss cheese, shredded
2 artichoke hearts, chopped
   Salt and pepper
1 tablespoon butter

Cheese Sauce:
2 tablespoons butter
2 tablespoons flour
1 cup milk
½ teaspoon salt
   Dash cayenne pepper
¼ cup Swiss cheese, shredded

1. To prepare Cheese Sauce, melt butter in a saucepan. Stir in flour. Cook 2 minutes over medium heat. Add milk and cook, stirring until sauce is thickened. Cook 5 minutes, stirring. Add remaining ingredients. Heat until cheese has melted.

2. To prepare omelets, thoroughly beat eggs with cream, salt and pepper.

3. Melt butter in an 8-inch omelet pan. Add eggs. Cook over medium heat until eggs are softly set.

4. Sprinkle ham, cheese and artichoke hearts over half of egg mixture. Fold omelet in half.

5. Heat through. Serve immediately with Cheese Sauce.

Serves 2.

CREAMY CUCUMBER SOUP

2 medium cucumbers, peeled and sliced
4 large green onions with most of greens, coarsely chopped
½ cup water
1 teaspoon salt
¼ teaspoon pepper
¾ cup potato, cooked and riced
3 sprigs fresh mint
1 cup chicken broth
½ cup heavy cream
   Chopped cucumber
   Fresh mint

1. Combine first 5 ingredients in a saucepan and simmer for 20 minutes. Cool; add to blender container.

2. Blend on high speed for 15 seconds, add potato. Cover and blend on high. Remove center of cover and with blender still on add remaining ingredients.

3. Serve chilled, garnished with chopped cucumber and fresh mint.

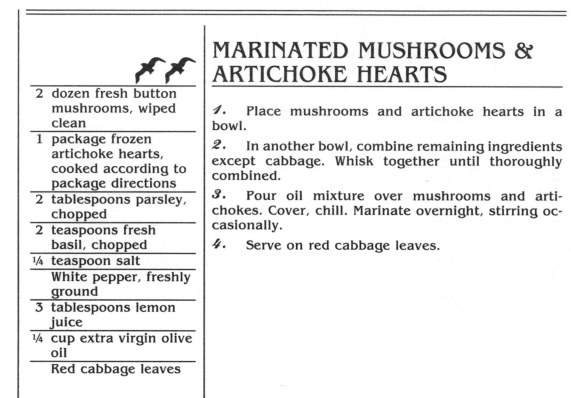

MARINATED MUSHROOMS & ARTICHOKE HEARTS

2	dozen fresh button mushrooms, wiped clean
1	package frozen artichoke hearts, cooked according to package directions
2	tablespoons parsley, chopped
2	teaspoons fresh basil, chopped
¼	teaspoon salt
	White pepper, freshly ground
3	tablespoons lemon juice
¼	cup extra virgin olive oil
	Red cabbage leaves

1. Place mushrooms and artichoke hearts in a bowl.

2. In another bowl, combine remaining ingredients except cabbage. Whisk together until thoroughly combined.

3. Pour oil mixture over mushrooms and artichokes. Cover, chill. Marinate overnight, stirring occasionally.

4. Serve on red cabbage leaves.

CHOCOLATE-ORANGE TRUFFLES

5	ounces semisweet chocolate
1	egg yolk
½	teaspoon orange rind, grated
1	cup plus 3 tablespoons pecans, finely chopped
2	tablespoons unsalted butter
2½	teaspoons Grand Marnier

1. In a double boiler, melt chocolate over hot, not simmering, water.

2. Turn chocolate into a bowl and add egg yolk, orange zest, 3 tablespoons pecans, butter and Grand Marnier. Beat together until thoroughly combined. Refrigerate until somewhat firm, at least 1 hour.

3. Spread remaining pecans on a sheet of waxed paper. Shape chocolate mixture into 1-inch balls and roll in pecans. Serve in individual paper or foil cups.

MUSSELS IN SNAIL BUTTER

24 mussels
½ cup butter, softened
2 tablespoons parsley, minced
6 cloves garlic, minced
1 tablespoon lemon juice
Salt and pepper

Oven temperature: 325°

1. Remove byssus threads, scrub clean, and steam mussels in covered pot in ½ cup water or white wine for 5–7 minutes, or until shells have opened. Remove from shells.

2. Preheat oven to 325°. Cream together butter, parsley, garlic, salt and pepper.

3. Put each mussel on a half shell, dot with snail butter and bake until butter is melted.

4. Serve immediately with French bread.

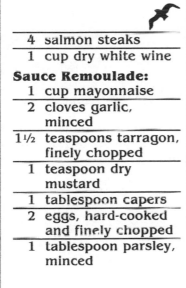

COLD POACHED SALMON WITH SAUCE REMOULADE

4 salmon steaks
1 cup dry white wine

Sauce Remoulade:
1 cup mayonnaise
2 cloves garlic, minced
1½ teaspoons tarragon, finely chopped
1 teaspoon dry mustard
1 tablespoon capers
2 eggs, hard-cooked and finely chopped
1 tablespoon parsley, minced

1. Put 1 inch of water in fry pan; add wine and bring to boil.

2. Add salmon steaks and cook 10 minutes per inch of thickness.

3. Drain and chill 4 hours or overnight.

4. To prepare Sauce Remoulade: Combine all ingredients; mix thoroughly. Let stand 2–3 hours before serving.

4. Serve chilled salmon with Sauce Remoulade. Garnish with fresh dill.

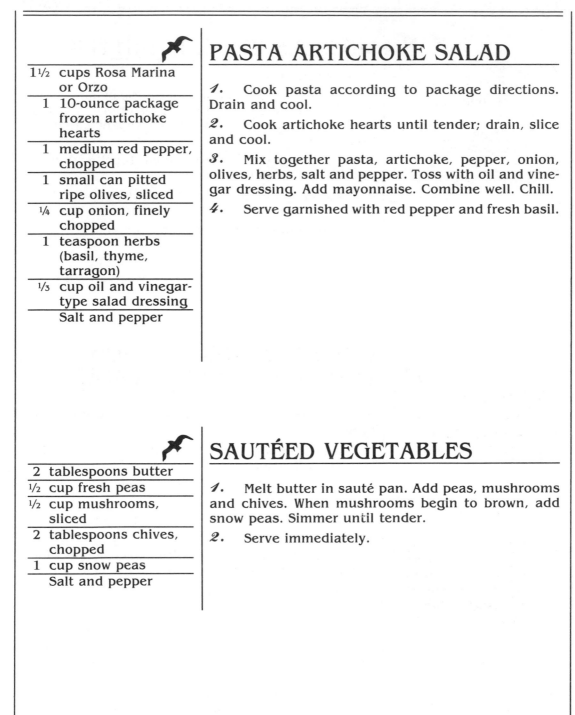

PASTA ARTICHOKE SALAD

1½ cups Rosa Marina
      or Orzo

1 10-ounce package
   frozen artichoke
   hearts

1 medium red pepper,
   chopped

1 small can pitted
   ripe olives, sliced

¼ cup onion, finely
   chopped

1 teaspoon herbs
   (basil, thyme,
   tarragon)

⅓ cup oil and vinegar-
   type salad dressing
   Salt and pepper

1. Cook pasta according to package directions. Drain and cool.

2. Cook artichoke hearts until tender; drain, slice and cool.

3. Mix together pasta, artichoke, pepper, onion, olives, herbs, salt and pepper. Toss with oil and vinegar dressing. Add mayonnaise. Combine well. Chill.

4. Serve garnished with red pepper and fresh basil.

SAUTÉED VEGETABLES

2 tablespoons butter

½ cup fresh peas

½ cup mushrooms,
   sliced

2 tablespoons chives,
   chopped

1 cup snow peas
   Salt and pepper

1. Melt butter in sauté pan. Add peas, mushrooms and chives. When mushrooms begin to brown, add snow peas. Simmer until tender.

2. Serve immediately.

BLUEBERRIES IN LEMON CREAM

2 cups blueberries, rinsed, drained and stems removed
1 pint whole milk
2 eggs, separated
½ cup granulated sugar
2 tablespoons flour
1 teaspoon lemon rind, grated

1. Bring milk to a boil in the top of a double boiler.

2. Beat the egg yolks and mix with ¼ cup sugar and the flour. Stir into the hot milk. Continue to stir until thickened. Strain immediately.

3. Beat egg whites until very stiff and add the remaining ¼ cup sugar. Beat until thoroughly combined. Stir into the custard mixture. Add lemon rind. Mix.

4. Put ½ cup blueberries into each of 4 individual dishes. Pour custard over berries.

BLOODY MARY

4 ounces Vodka
3 cups V-8 juice
4 teaspoons lemon juice
Dash Tabasco sauce
1 teaspoon Worcestershire sauce
1½ teaspoons sugar
Dash dill

Combine all ingredients in pitcher with ice. Mix well. Serve over ice. Garnish with fresh celery, lime wedge, salt and freshly ground black pepper.

Yield: 1 pitcher.

EGGS ADRIENNE

8 tablespoons butter
8 eggs (do not scramble)
8 tablespoons cream cheese, cut in small pieces
2 tablespoons chives, chopped
Salt and freshly ground pepper

1. Melt butter in a 10-inch skillet over medium heat. Add eggs, being careful not to break yolks. Carefully add cream cheese, one piece at a time, at edge of skillet. Sprinkle with chopped chives, and salt and pepper to taste.

2. As cheese melts into butter, and egg whites begin to cook, gently spoon cheese mixture over egg yolks to cook.

3. Serve when eggs are cooked, and yolks are still soft.

MENU • III

Friday Dinner

★ Vichyssoise ★
★ Lobster Parisienne ★
★ Rice Pilaf ★
★ Lemon Green Beans ★
★ Raspberry Cheesecake ★

Saturday Breakfast

Fresh Papaya
★ Scrambled Eggs with Smoked Salmon ★
Toasted Bagels
★ Tomato Slices with Red Onion ★

Saturday Lunch

★ Seviche ★
★ Rice Salad ★
★ Garden Salad with Creamy Bleu Cheese Dressing ★
★ Chocolate/Cheese Brownies ★

Saturday Dinner

Oysters on the Half Shell
★ Chilled Roast Tenderloin of Beef ★
★ Russian Salad ★
★ Asparagus Vinaigrette ★
French Rolls
★ Almond Pound Cake ★
★ Strawberries Romanoff ★

Sunday Brunch

★ Smoked Trout with Horseradish Sauce ★
★ Tomato and Basil Quiche ★
Buttercrunch Lettuce with Lemon Vinaigrette
★ Coconut Delights ★

VICHYSSOISE

½ small onion, sliced
1½ cups chicken broth
1½ cups potato, cooked and diced
⅛ teaspoon white pepper
1 cup cracked ice
½ cup heavy cream
Chopped chives

1. Place onion and ½ cup chicken broth in blender container. Cover and blend on high speed for 10 seconds.

2. Remove cover and add potato, remaining chicken broth and pepper. Cover and blend on high for 10 seconds.

3. Remove cover and add ice and cream. Cover, blend 10 seconds longer.

4. Chill. Serve garnished with chopped chives.

LOBSTER PARISIENNE

4 lobsters, 1¼–1½ pounds, boiled
1 tablespoon butter
1 medium tomato, peeled, seeded and chopped
1 tablespoon chives, chopped
¼ cup champagne
¼ cup heavy cream
Salt, freshly ground white pepper
Parsley

1. Remove cooked lobster meat from shell and cut into large chunks. Reserve shell from tail and body sections.

2. Melt butter in sauté pan. Add tomato, chives and lobster meat; heat through.

3. Add champagne. Reduce liquids to about 1 tablespoon.

4. Add cream. Cook until liquid is reduced by half and thickened. Add salt and pepper.

5. Return lobster with sauce to shells. Garnish with fresh parsley. Serve immediately.

RICE PILAF

2 tablespoons butter
1 medium onion, chopped
1 teaspoon tarragon
2½ cups chicken broth
1¼ cups uncooked rice
½ teaspoon salt
White pepper, freshly ground

1. In a saucepan, melt butter; add onion and tarragon. Cook until onion is soft and golden, but not brown.

2. Add rice, salt, pepper and chicken broth; bring to boiling. Reduce heat and simmer for 25–30 minutes or until all liquid is absorbed and rice is tender.

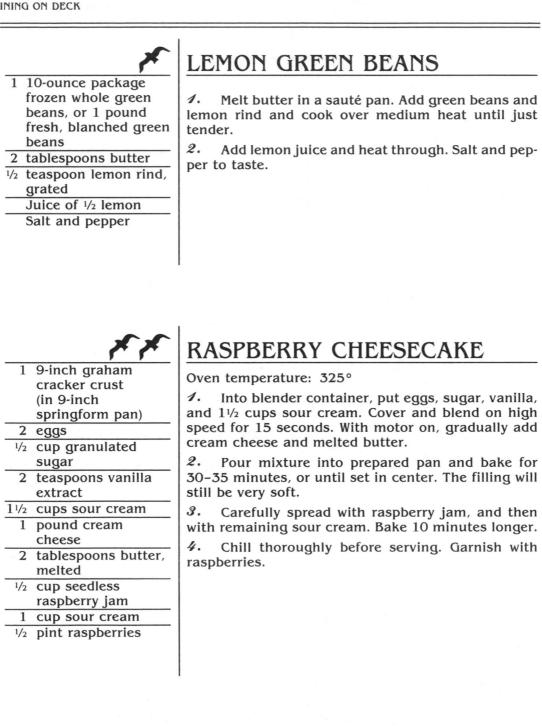

LEMON GREEN BEANS

1 10-ounce package frozen whole green beans, or 1 pound fresh, blanched green beans

2 tablespoons butter

½ teaspoon lemon rind, grated

Juice of ½ lemon

Salt and pepper

1. Melt butter in a sauté pan. Add green beans and lemon rind and cook over medium heat until just tender.

2. Add lemon juice and heat through. Salt and pepper to taste.

RASPBERRY CHEESECAKE

1 9-inch graham cracker crust (in 9-inch springform pan)

2 eggs

½ cup granulated sugar

2 teaspoons vanilla extract

1½ cups sour cream

1 pound cream cheese

2 tablespoons butter, melted

½ cup seedless raspberry jam

1 cup sour cream

½ pint raspberries

Oven temperature: 325°

1. Into blender container, put eggs, sugar, vanilla, and 1½ cups sour cream. Cover and blend on high speed for 15 seconds. With motor on, gradually add cream cheese and melted butter.

2. Pour mixture into prepared pan and bake for 30–35 minutes, or until set in center. The filling will still be very soft.

3. Carefully spread with raspberry jam, and then with remaining sour cream. Bake 10 minutes longer.

4. Chill thoroughly before serving. Garnish with raspberries.

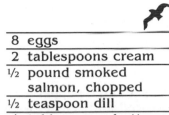

SCRAMBLED EGGS WITH SMOKED SALMON

8 eggs
2 tablespoons cream
½ pound smoked salmon, chopped
½ teaspoon dill
4 tablespoons butter
3 ounces cream cheese, cut in chunks

1. Beat eggs with cream. Add smoked salmon and dill.

2. Melt butter in fry pan. Pour in egg mixture, stirring. As eggs begin to cook, add cream cheese. Continue cooking and stirring gently until eggs mound and are soft, but not dry.

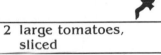

TOMATO SLICES WITH RED ONION

2 large tomatoes, sliced
1 medium red onion, thinly sliced
½ teaspoon basil
1 tablespoon chives, chopped
2 tablespoons red wine vinegar
½ cup extra virgin olive oil
1 tablespoon parsley, chopped

1. Arrange tomato slices in a shallow serving dish, such as a quiche pan. Layer onion slices on top.

2. Combine remaining ingredients thoroughly with a whisk, or shake well. Pour over tomatoes and onions. Chill.

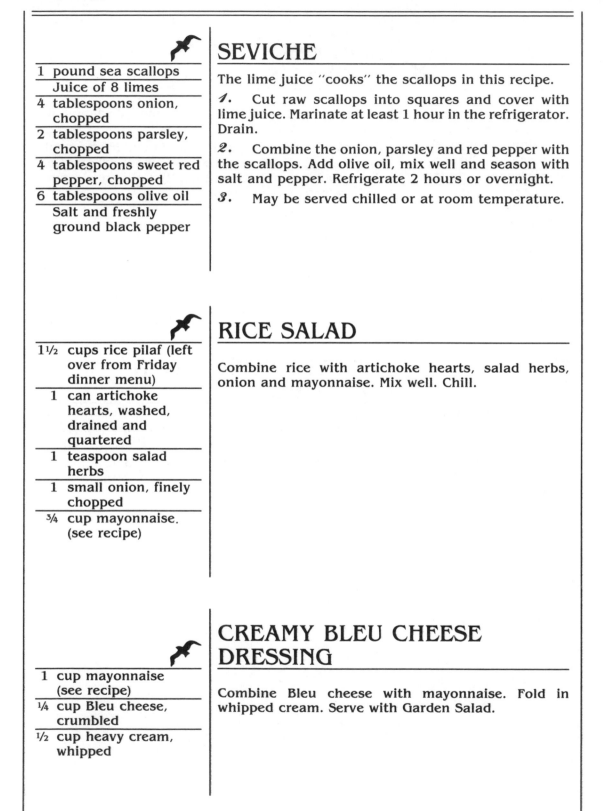

SEVICHE

The lime juice "cooks" the scallops in this recipe.

1. Cut raw scallops into squares and cover with lime juice. Marinate at least 1 hour in the refrigerator. Drain.

2. Combine the onion, parsley and red pepper with the scallops. Add olive oil, mix well and season with salt and pepper. Refrigerate 2 hours or overnight.

3. May be served chilled or at room temperature.

1 pound sea scallops
Juice of 8 limes
4 tablespoons onion, chopped
2 tablespoons parsley, chopped
4 tablespoons sweet red pepper, chopped
6 tablespoons olive oil
Salt and freshly ground black pepper

RICE SALAD

Combine rice with artichoke hearts, salad herbs, onion and mayonnaise. Mix well. Chill.

1½ cups rice pilaf (left over from Friday dinner menu)
1 can artichoke hearts, washed, drained and quartered
1 teaspoon salad herbs
1 small onion, finely chopped
¾ cup mayonnaise. (see recipe)

CREAMY BLEU CHEESE DRESSING

Combine Bleu cheese with mayonnaise. Fold in whipped cream. Serve with Garden Salad.

1 cup mayonnaise (see recipe)
¼ cup Bleu cheese, crumbled
½ cup heavy cream, whipped

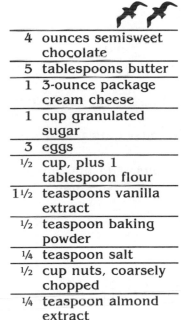

CHOCOLATE-CHEESE BROWNIES

Oven temperature: 350°

4 ounces semisweet chocolate
5 tablespoons butter
1 3-ounce package cream cheese
1 cup granulated sugar
3 eggs
½ cup, plus 1 tablespoon flour
1½ teaspoons vanilla extract
½ teaspoon baking powder
¼ teaspoon salt
½ cup nuts, coarsely chopped
¼ teaspoon almond extract

1. Melt chocolate and 3 tablespoons butter over very low heat, stirring constantly. Set aside and cool. Cream remaining butter with cream cheese until softened. Gradually add ¼ cup sugar, creaming until light and fluffy. Blend in 1 egg, 1 tablespoon flour, and ½ teaspoon vanilla. Set aside.

2. Beat remaining eggs until thick and light in color. Gradually add remaining ¾ cup sugar, beating until thickened. Add baking powder, salt, and remaining ½ cup flour. Blend in cooled chocolate mixture, nuts, almond extract, and remaining 1 teaspoon vanilla. Measure 1 cup chocolate batter and set aside.

3. Spread remaining chocolate batter in a greased 9-inch square pan. Top with cheese mixture. Drop reserved chocolate batter from tablespoon onto cheese mixture; swirl with spatula to marble.

4. Bake at 350° for 35–40 minutes. Cool; then cut. Cover and store in refrigerator.

Yield: 20 brownies.

CHILLED ROAST TENDERLOIN OF BEEF

Oven temperature: 350°

1 1½–2 pound beef tenderloin roast, trimmed and peeled
6–8 cloves garlic
2 tablespoons Dijon-style mustard
2 tablespoons grated horseradish
Cherry tomatoes
Fresh parsley

1. Split garlic cloves in half, lengthwise. Make slits in beef. Insert garlic into slits. Spread beef with a mixture of mustard and horseradish.

2. Roast tenderloin for 30–40 minutes or to 120° on a meat thermometer for rare. Chill. Serve garnished with cherry tomatoes and fresh parsley.

RUSSIAN SALAD

4 medium new
potatoes, quartered
¾ cup tiny frozen peas
4 carrots, chopped
½ cup onion, finely
chopped
¼ cup parsley, minced
Salt and pepper
½ cup mayonnaise
(see recipe)
Fresh parsley
to garnish

1. Cook potatoes in boiling water; peel, cool and dice.

2. Cook peas according to package directions. Drain and cool.

3. Cook carrots in boiling water until just tender. Cool.

4. Combine first 6 ingredients. Add mayonnaise. Combine well. Chill. Garnish with fresh parsley.

ASPARAGUS VINAIGRETTE

1 pound fresh
asparagus
½ cup extra virgin olive
oil
3 tablespoons lemon
juice
1 tablespoon garlic,
minced
¼ teaspoon tarragon
¼ teaspoon chives
¼ teaspoon basil

1. Break off tough stalks from asparagus. Wash. Steam for 5–8 minutes, until tender, but not soft.

2. Combine next 6 ingredients. Shake well. Pour over asparagus. Chill several hours or overnight.

STRAWBERRIES ROMANOFF

2 cups fresh
strawberries, sliced
¼ cup Kirsch
Whipped cream
Fresh mint leaves

1. Arrange strawberries in individual serving dishes; champagne glasses work well. Pour 1 tablespoon Kirsch over each serving.

2. Garnish with whipped cream and mint leaves.

NOTE: Whip cream at home and keep on ice in an airtight container. If cream should begin to separate, whip it back together with a wire whisk. It works very well.

ALMOND POUND CAKE

1 cup butter, cut in pieces

1 cup granulated sugar

4 eggs, separated

2 teaspoons almond extract

1 teaspoon vanilla extract

½ teaspoon salt

¼ teaspoon baking powder

2 cups all-purpose flour

(This recipe may be made quickly in your food processor.)

Oven temperature: 300°

1. With metal blade in place, add butter and ¾ cup sugar to the work bowl. Process, turning on and off, until mixture is creamed, about 15–20 seconds. Add egg yolks one at a time, and process after each addition until well combined. Add almond extract, vanilla, salt and baking powder. Process until combined, about 5 seconds. Add flour and quickly turn machine off and on until flour disappears.

2. In a bowl, beat egg whites until soft peaks form. Continue beating, gradually adding remaining ¼ cup sugar, until stiff, but not dry.

3. Pour batter from work bowl over egg whites and fold together carefully.

4. Pour into well-greased 6-cup loaf pan. Bake in a preheated 300° oven for 1¼–1½ hours, or until a toothpick inserted in the center comes out clean. Makes one cake.

SMOKED TROUT WITH HORSERADISH SAUCE

½ cup heavy cream, whipped

2 tablespoons grated horseradish

2 whole smoked trout, skinned, boned and halved

1 lemon, sliced

1 small red onion, sliced

Lettuce

1. Fold whipped cream together with horseradish.

2. Arrange trout on lettuce leaves on 4 individual serving plates. Garnish with lemon and red onion slices. Serve with Horseradish Sauce.

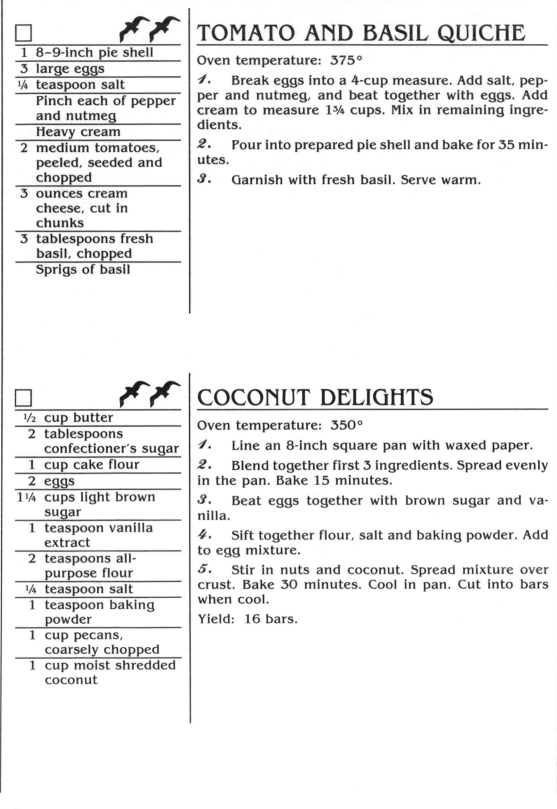

TOMATO AND BASIL QUICHE

☐

1 8–9-inch pie shell
3 large eggs
¼ teaspoon salt
Pinch each of pepper and nutmeg
Heavy cream
2 medium tomatoes, peeled, seeded and chopped
3 ounces cream cheese, cut in chunks
3 tablespoons fresh basil, chopped
Sprigs of basil

Oven temperature: 375°

1. Break eggs into a 4-cup measure. Add salt, pepper and nutmeg, and beat together with eggs. Add cream to measure 1¾ cups. Mix in remaining ingredients.

2. Pour into prepared pie shell and bake for 35 minutes.

3. Garnish with fresh basil. Serve warm.

COCONUT DELIGHTS

☐

½ cup butter
2 tablespoons confectioner's sugar
1 cup cake flour
2 eggs
1¼ cups light brown sugar
1 teaspoon vanilla extract
2 teaspoons all-purpose flour
¼ teaspoon salt
1 teaspoon baking powder
1 cup pecans, coarsely chopped
1 cup moist shredded coconut

Oven temperature: 350°

1. Line an 8-inch square pan with waxed paper.

2. Blend together first 3 ingredients. Spread evenly in the pan. Bake 15 minutes.

3. Beat eggs together with brown sugar and vanilla.

4. Sift together flour, salt and baking powder. Add to egg mixture.

5. Stir in nuts and coconut. Spread mixture over crust. Bake 30 minutes. Cool in pan. Cut into bars when cool.

Yield: 16 bars.

6

COOL WEATHER SAILING

The warming sun, crisp air and brisk breezes make spring and fall sailing wonderfully invigorating. Appetites are heightened by the refreshing air, as well as the extra energy expended to sail in a stiff wind. The air is aglow and tingly; at day's end you are very nearly exhausted, yet, too, exhilarated by the excitement of the day. Food becomes a mainstay to keeping up your strength and to staying warm. For cool weather sailing, breakfasts are generally heartier, and there is always something hot at lunch. Dinner is a time to huddle around the table in the main cabin, recount the day's adventure and those of days' past, and enjoy savory dishes, inspired by the coziness away from the elements. The mind-set is different and thus the food and dining details are different. The end result, however, is very much the same; a feeling of weary contentment, of elegance in simplicity, a closeness with nature.

MENU FOR A DAY SAIL

Breakfast

Grapefruit Half

★ French Toast with Maple Syrup ★

Sausage

Coffee

Lunch

★ Cream of Tomato Soup ★

Roast Beef with Red Onion
and Horseradish on Pumpernickel

★ Almond Spritz Cookies ★

Dinner

★ Lasagne ★

Garlic Bread

Tossed Salad

★ Chocolate Chestnut Brownies ★

FRENCH TOAST

8 slices white bread
3 eggs
1 cup heavy cream
1/8 teaspoon salt
1 teaspoon cinnamon
4 tablespoons butter
   Confectioner's sugar
   Pure maple syrup

1. Beat eggs together with cream, salt and cinnamon.

2. Melt butter in fry pan at medium-high temperature.

3. Dip bread in egg mixture to coat both sides. Place 2–3 slices bread in fry pan at once. Cook until golden brown on both sides. Repeat with remaining slices.

4. Sprinkle with confectioner's sugar. Serve with warm maple syrup.

CREAM OF TOMATO SOUP

12 very ripe tomatoes, peeled, cut up
1 cup water
1 cup celery, sliced
1/2 onion, sliced
1/4 cup fresh parsley, minced
3 tablespoons cornstarch
3 tablespoons butter, melted
2 tablespoons brown sugar
2 teaspoons salt
   Freshly ground pepper
2 cups heavy cream
1 egg yolk, beaten
   Chives, chopped

1. Simmer tomatoes, water, celery, onion and parsley for 30 minutes. Puree and strain.

2. Mix together cornstarch and butter. Stir into soup to thicken over medium heat.

3. Add brown sugar, salt and pepper. (Soup may be frozen at this time, if desired.)

4. Stir cream and egg yolk together, then into very hot soup.

5. Serve hot, garnished with chopped chives.

ALMOND SPRITZ COOKIES

1 cup butter, softened
½ cup granulated sugar
1 egg
1 teaspoon almond extract
2 cups all-purpose flour
¼ cup ground almonds
½ teaspoon salt

Oven temperature: 400°

1. Cream butter and sugar. Beat in egg and almond extract. Add flour, ground almonds and salt. Mix thoroughly.

2. Place dough in cookie press. Form desired shapes on ungreased baking sheet.

3. Bake in a preheated oven for 6–9 minutes. Immediately remove cookies from baking sheet to wire rack.

Yield: 5 dozen cookies.

LASAGNE

½ pound lasagne noodles
½ pound ground beef
1 tablespoon olive oil
½ pound Italian sausage, cut in 8 pieces
2 eggs, hard-cooked, peeled and sliced
4 ounces mozzarella cheese, thinly sliced
1 cup ricotta cheese
¾ cup Parmesan cheese, freshly grated
2 cups spaghetti sauce, following recipe, or from a jar

Oven temperature: 325°

1. Prepare spaghetti sauce.

2. Cook noodles according to package directions; rinse in cold water. Drain. Set aside.

3. Sauté ground beef in olive oil, breaking into small pieces as it cooks. Add to spaghetti sauce.

4. In a deep 8-inch square pan, pour ⅔ cup sauce mixture. Cover with 2–3 noodles, cut to fit pan. Spread with ½ cup ricotta cheese. Layer with ½ the slices of mozzarella and the slices of one egg. Sprinkle with ¼ cup Parmesan cheese. Pour ⅔ cup sauce over all. Repeat to form another layer.

5. Arrange sausage on top of second layer. Sprinkle all with remaining ¼ cup Parmesan cheese.

6. Bake in preheated oven 45–50 minutes. Cool.

7. Refrigerate or freeze.

8. Bring to room temperature and reheat in a medium oven for 30 minutes before serving.

SPAGHETTI SAUCE

1 cup mushrooms, sliced
1 large onion, chopped
2 tablespoons olive oil
3 pounds fresh tomatoes, quartered
¼ cup water
4 tablespoons tomato paste
2 tablespoons basil, chopped
1 tablespoon oregano, chopped

1. Sauté onions and mushrooms in olive oil. Set aside.

2. Put tomatoes and water in a 5–6 quart saucepan. Cook over medium heat until tomatoes have cooked down and are reduced by half.

3. Add onion, mushrooms, and remaining ingredients to tomatoes.

4. Simmer slowly, uncovered for 1 hour.

CHOCOLATE CHESTNUT BROWNIES

4 eggs
1¾ cups granulated sugar
½ cup butter, melted
5 ounces unsweetened chocolate, melted
1 8¾-ounce can chestnut spread
1 teaspoon vanilla extract
1 scant cup flour
½ teaspoon baking powder
½ teaspoon salt
Confectioner's sugar

Chestnut spread is available at specialty stores.

Oven temperature: 350°

1. Beat together eggs, sugar, butter, chocolate and chestnut spread.

2. Add vanilla, flour, baking powder, and salt, mixing after each addition.

3. Pour into a greased and floured 9 x 13-inch pan. Bake 30 minutes. Sprinkle with confectioner's sugar.

4. Let cool for 45 minutes before cutting.

Yield: 2 dozen brownies.

MENU FOR A WEEKEND SAIL

Saturday Breakfast

★ Tomato Juice (see page 87) ★

★ Corned Beef Hash ★

Poached Eggs

★ Corn Muffins ★

Coffee

Saturday Lunch

★ New England-Style Clam Chowder ★

Bacon, Lettuce & Tomato Sandwiches

Saturday Dinner

★ Coq au Vin ★

Tossed Salad

★ French Bread (see page 100) ★

★ Apricot Pound Cake (see page 46) ★

Sunday Breakfast

Orange Juice

★ Western Omelet ★

★ Toasted Herb Bread (see page 97) ★

Coffee

Sunday Lunch

★ Mushroom Bisque ★

★ Crabmeat Salad & Sprouts in a Pocket ★

Fresh Fruit

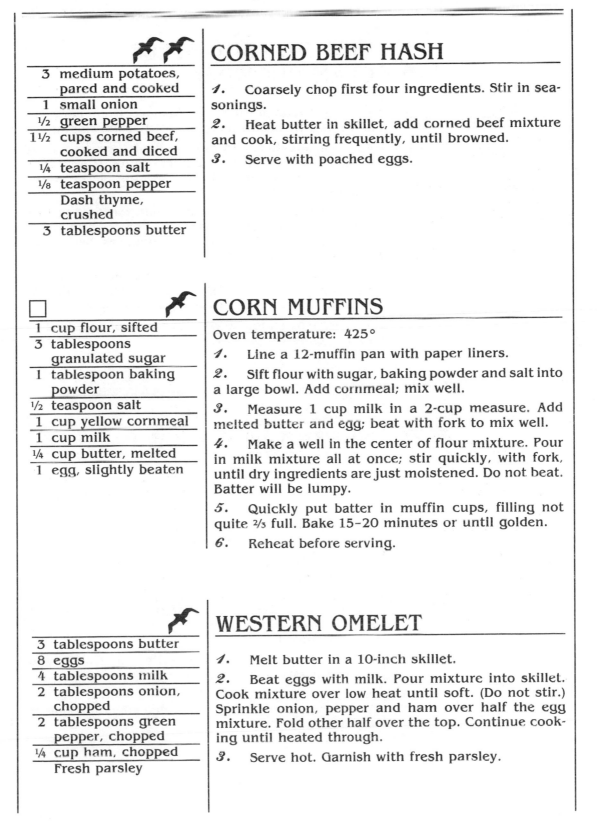

CORNED BEEF HASH

3 medium potatoes, pared and cooked
1 small onion
½ green pepper
1½ cups corned beef, cooked and diced
¼ teaspoon salt
⅛ teaspoon pepper
Dash thyme, crushed
3 tablespoons butter

1. Coarsely chop first four ingredients. Stir in seasonings.

2. Heat butter in skillet, add corned beef mixture and cook, stirring frequently, until browned.

3. Serve with poached eggs.

CORN MUFFINS

1 cup flour, sifted
3 tablespoons granulated sugar
1 tablespoon baking powder
½ teaspoon salt
1 cup yellow cornmeal
1 cup milk
¼ cup butter, melted
1 egg, slightly beaten

Oven temperature: 425°

1. Line a 12-muffin pan with paper liners.

2. Sift flour with sugar, baking powder and salt into a large bowl. Add cornmeal; mix well.

3. Measure 1 cup milk in a 2-cup measure. Add melted butter and egg; beat with fork to mix well.

4. Make a well in the center of flour mixture. Pour in milk mixture all at once; stir quickly, with fork, until dry ingredients are just moistened. Do not beat. Batter will be lumpy.

5. Quickly put batter in muffin cups, filling not quite ⅔ full. Bake 15–20 minutes or until golden.

6. Reheat before serving.

WESTERN OMELET

3 tablespoons butter
8 eggs
4 tablespoons milk
2 tablespoons onion, chopped
2 tablespoons green pepper, chopped
¼ cup ham, chopped
Fresh parsley

1. Melt butter in a 10-inch skillet.

2. Beat eggs with milk. Pour mixture into skillet. Cook mixture over low heat until soft. (Do not stir.) Sprinkle onion, pepper and ham over half the egg mixture. Fold other half over the top. Continue cooking until heated through.

3. Serve hot. Garnish with fresh parsley.

NEW ENGLAND-STYLE CLAM CHOWDER

4 slices bacon, finely chopped
1 medium onion, finely chopped
2 medium potatoes
Salt
Freshly ground white pepper
2 cups heavy cream
5 10-ounce cans of minced clams with broth reserved
Thyme
Paprika
Parsley, chopped

1. Fry bacon until crisp. Remove from pan. Set aside. Lightly brown onion in hot bacon drippings.

2. Peel and dice potatoes and cook them in boiling water to just cover until tender, about 10–15 minutes. Remove potatoes from pan and let the water cool down a bit.

3. Combine the bacon, onion, potatoes and potato water in a saucepan, and add clam broth. Bring mixture to a boil and simmer for 5 minutes. Season to taste with salt and pepper.

4. Gradually add the cream. When liquid reaches the boiling point, add clams. Let clams heat through. Sprinkle with a pinch of finely rubbed thyme.

5. Serve in heated bowls with a dash of paprika and a bit of chopped parsley.

MUSHROOM BISQUE

½ pound mushrooms
2 cups chicken broth
1 small onion, chopped
4 tablespoons butter
3 tablespoons flour
1½ cups milk
½ cup heavy cream
Salt
Freshly ground white pepper
Cayenne pepper
Paprika
1 tablespoon sherry

1. Clean mushrooms and cut off stems. Slice 4 cups and reserve. Discard any dried ends from stems. Finely chop remaining caps and stems.

2. Place chicken broth, chopped mushrooms, and onion in a saucepan. Simmer, covered, 20 minutes.

3. Sauté reserved mushrooms in 1 tablespoon butter and reserve for garnish.

4. Melt remaining butter in a saucepan; add flour and stir with a wire whisk until blended. Add milk to flour mixture and cook, stirring, until thickened and smooth. Add cream.

5. Combine mushroom broth with white sauce and season to taste with salt, pepper and cayenne pepper.

6. Before serving, reheat and add sherry. Serve in heated cups garnished with sautéed mushroom slices and dash paprika.

COQ AU VIN

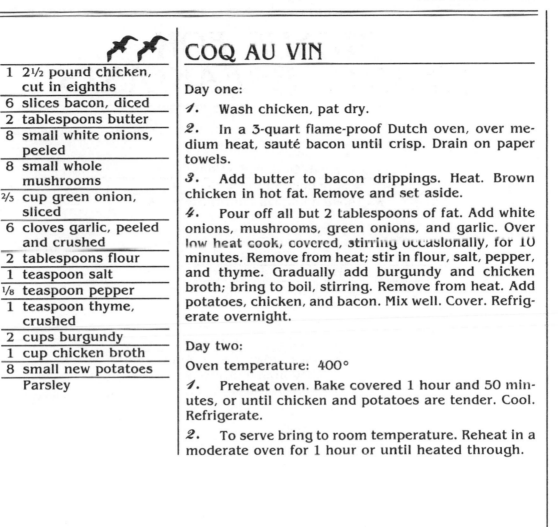

1	2½ pound chicken, cut in eighths
6	slices bacon, diced
2	tablespoons butter
8	small white onions, peeled
8	small whole mushrooms
⅔	cup green onion, sliced
6	cloves garlic, peeled and crushed
2	tablespoons flour
1	teaspoon salt
⅛	teaspoon pepper
1	teaspoon thyme, crushed
2	cups burgundy
1	cup chicken broth
8	small new potatoes
	Parsley

Day one:

1. Wash chicken, pat dry.

2. In a 3-quart flame-proof Dutch oven, over medium heat, sauté bacon until crisp. Drain on paper towels.

3. Add butter to bacon drippings. Heat. Brown chicken in hot fat. Remove and set aside.

4. Pour off all but 2 tablespoons of fat. Add white onions, mushrooms, green onions, and garlic. Over low heat cook, covered, stirring occasionally, for 10 minutes. Remove from heat; stir in flour, salt, pepper, and thyme. Gradually add burgundy and chicken broth; bring to boil, stirring. Remove from heat. Add potatoes, chicken, and bacon. Mix well. Cover. Refrigerate overnight.

Day two:

Oven temperature: 400°

1. Preheat oven. Bake covered 1 hour and 50 minutes, or until chicken and potatoes are tender. Cool. Refrigerate.

2. To serve bring to room temperature. Reheat in a moderate oven for 1 hour or until heated through.

CRABMEAT SALAD POCKETS

1	pound crabmeat
¾	cup celery, finely chopped
2	tablespoons lemon juice
1	teaspoon salt
⅛	teaspoon pepper
¼	cup mayonnaise
1	teaspoon capers
	Alfalfa sprouts
4	pita breads

1. Remove any cartilage from crabmeat.

2. Put celery in a bowl. Mix in lemon juice, salt, pepper, mayonnaise, and capers.

3. Add crabmeat and mix gently, but thoroughly. Refrigerate until serving.

4. Serve in pita bread pockets with alfalfa sprouts.

MENUS FOR HEARTY BREAKFASTS

Fresh Orange Sections
★ Creamed Chipped Beef ★
★ Toasted English Muffin Bread ★

Grapefruit Juice
★ Hearty Ham and Egg Scramble ★
★ Baking Powder Biscuits ★

Cantaloupe with Lime
Hot Oatmeal with Brown Sugar and Cream
★ Nutty Bran Muffins ★

Apricot Juice
★ Buttery Waffles with Blueberry Syrup ★
Bacon

★ Grenadine Grapefruit ★
★ Sautéed Mushrooms ★
English Muffins

Green Seedless Grapes
★ Lemon Pancakes ★
★ Frizzled Ham ★

★ Pan Fried Steak ★
Fried Eggs
★ Home-Style Potatoes ★
Toasted Whole Grain Bread

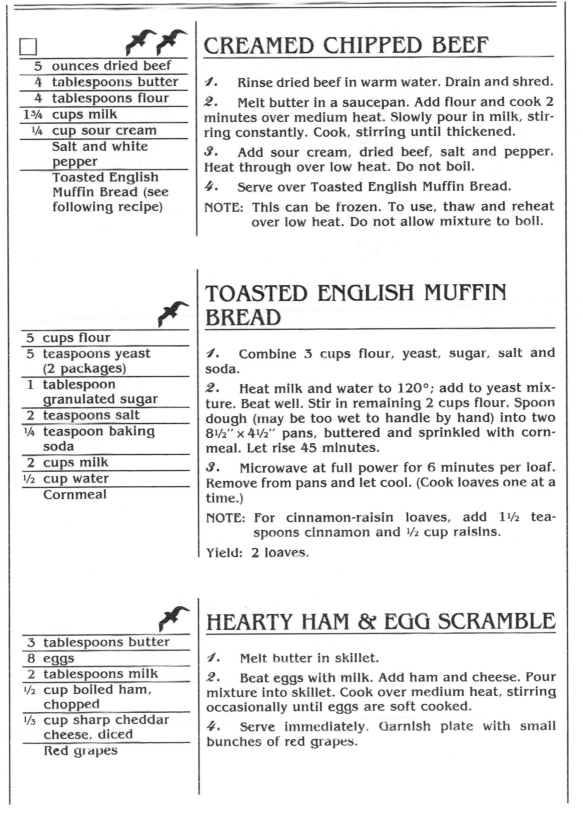

CREAMED CHIPPED BEEF

5 ounces dried beef
4 tablespoons butter
4 tablespoons flour
1¾ cups milk
¼ cup sour cream
Salt and white pepper
Toasted English Muffin Bread (see following recipe)

1. Rinse dried beef in warm water. Drain and shred.

2. Melt butter in a saucepan. Add flour and cook 2 minutes over medium heat. Slowly pour in milk, stirring constantly. Cook, stirring until thickened.

3. Add sour cream, dried beef, salt and pepper. Heat through over low heat. Do not boil.

4. Serve over Toasted English Muffin Bread.

NOTE: This can be frozen. To use, thaw and reheat over low heat. Do not allow mixture to boil.

TOASTED ENGLISH MUFFIN BREAD

5 cups flour
5 teaspoons yeast (2 packages)
1 tablespoon granulated sugar
2 teaspoons salt
¼ teaspoon baking soda
2 cups milk
½ cup water
Cornmeal

1. Combine 3 cups flour, yeast, sugar, salt and soda.

2. Heat milk and water to 120°; add to yeast mixture. Beat well. Stir in remaining 2 cups flour. Spoon dough (may be too wet to handle by hand) into two 8½'' x 4½'' pans, buttered and sprinkled with cornmeal. Let rise 45 minutes.

3. Microwave at full power for 6 minutes per loaf. Remove from pans and let cool. (Cook loaves one at a time.)

NOTE: For cinnamon-raisin loaves, add 1½ teaspoons cinnamon and ½ cup raisins.

Yield: 2 loaves.

HEARTY HAM & EGG SCRAMBLE

3 tablespoons butter
8 eggs
2 tablespoons milk
½ cup boiled ham, chopped
⅓ cup sharp cheddar cheese, diced
Red grapes

1. Melt butter in skillet.

2. Beat eggs with milk. Add ham and cheese. Pour mixture into skillet. Cook over medium heat, stirring occasionally until eggs are soft cooked.

4. Serve immediately. Garnish plate with small bunches of red grapes.

NUTTY BRAN MUFFINS

1	cup all-purpose flour
2	teaspoons baking powder
½	teaspoon baking soda
1	teaspoon salt
3	cups bran cereal
½	cup seedless raisins
⅓	cup pecans, coarsely chopped
⅓	cup shortening
½	cup granulated sugar
1	egg
1	cup buttermilk

Oven temperature: 400°

1. Line muffin pan cups with paper liners.

2. Sift flour with baking powder, soda and salt into a medium bowl. Add bran, raisins and pecans. Mix well.

3. In large mixer bowl, cream shortening with sugar until light and fluffy. Beat in egg.

4. Using fork, stir flour mixture into shortening mixture alternating with buttermilk, stirring only until dry ingredients are moistened. Batter will be lumpy.

5. Spoon batter into muffin pan cups, filling about ⅔ full. Bake 20–25 minutes, or until golden.

6. Serve hot.

BAKING POWDER BISCUITS

2	cups all-purpose flour
3	teaspoons baking powder
1	teaspoon salt
⅓	cup shortening
¾	cup milk

Oven temperature: 450°

1. In a medium bowl, sift flour with baking powder and salt.

2. Cut shortening into flour mixture with a pastry blender until mixture resembles coarse oatmeal.

3. Make a well in the center. Pour in milk all at once. Stir quickly with a fork until dough leaves sides of bowl and forms a ball.

4. Turn dough out onto a lightly floured surface. Gently knead 6 or 8 times.

5. Gently roll out dough to ½- to ¾-inch thickness.

6. Using a floured 2½-inch biscuit cutter, cut straight down into dough.

7. Place on ungreased baking sheet; bake 12–15 minutes.

BUTTERY WAFFLES

4 eggs
2 cups all-purpose flour
1 teaspoon salt
1 teaspoon baking soda
1 teaspoon baking powder
1 cup milk
1 cup sour cream
1 cup butter, melted

1. Preheat waffle iron.

2. Beat eggs until light.

3. Sift together flour, salt, soda and baking powder.

4. Mix milk and sour cream.

5. Add flour mixture and milk mixture alternately to beaten eggs, beginning and ending with flour mixture. Add melted butter and blend thoroughly.

6. For each waffle, pour batter into center of lower half of waffle iron until it spreads to 1 inch from edge—about ½ cup.

7. Lower iron cover on batter; cook as manufacturer directs, or until waffle iron stops steaming.

8. Carefully loosen edge of waffle with fork; remove.

9. Cool. Place waxed paper between waffles. Freeze in airtight container.

10. To serve, remove from freezer and toast until heated through.

GRENADINE GRAPEFRUIT

2 grapefruit, halved and sections separated
4 tablespoons Grenadine

Sprinkle each grapefruit half with 1 tablespoon Grenadine. Serve cold.

SAUTÉED MUSHROOMS ON ENGLISH MUFFINS

4 tablespoons butter
1 pound mushrooms, thinly sliced
  Salt and pepper
  Worcestershire sauce
  Chives

1.   Melt butter in skillet. Sauté mushrooms, stirring frequently with a wooden spoon, for several minutes or until they are lightly colored, but still crisp. Season with salt and pepper and a dash of Worcestershire sauce.

2.   Serve on English muffins, split, buttered and toasted. Sprinkle with chives. Serve with crisp strips of bacon.

LEMON PANCAKES

2 cups flour
2½ tablespoons granulated sugar
1½ tablespoons baking powder
½ teaspoon salt
2 egg yolks
2½ cups milk
2 tablespoons butter, melted
  Rind of 1 lemon, grated
2 tablespoons lemon juice
2 egg whites, beaten until they hold soft peaks
  Butter
  Warm honey
  Frizzled Ham (see following recipe)

1.   In a bowl, sift flour with sugar, baking powder and salt.

2.   In a separate bowl, beat egg yolks and stir in milk, melted butter, lemon rind and lemon juice. Stir liquid into flour mixture until just moistened. Batter will be lumpy. Fold in egg whites.

3.   Drop batter by tablespoons onto hot oiled skillet and cook until they are bubbling on the surface. Turn and brown on other side.

4.   Serve pancakes immediately with butter and warm honey, and Frizzled Ham.

FRIZZLED HAM

2 tablespoons butter
8 thin slices boiled ham
  Parsley

1. Melt butter in skillet. Add ham and sauté until edges begin to curl and ham darkens in color.

2. If desired, fold slices in thirds and garnish with parsley.

3. Serve with Lemon Pancakes or other breakfast foods.

PAN FRIED STEAK

4 small delmonico or
  rib-eye steaks
4 tablespoons butter
1 tablespoon chives,
  chopped
1 tablespoon brandy

1. Melt butter in a skillet. Add steaks and chives. Sauté steaks 3 minutes per side. Add brandy and cook 2 minutes over high heat.

2. Serve steaks immediately with fried eggs and Home-Style Potatoes (see following recipe).

HOME-STYLE POTATOES

3 tablespoons butter
1 medium onion,
  chopped
3 potatoes, baked,
  peeled and diced
2 tablespoons parsley,
  chopped
  Salt and pepper
2 teaspoons paprika

1. Melt butter in a skillet. Add onion; cook 5 minutes or until soft. Add potatoes, parsley, salt and pepper to taste and paprika.

2. Sauté mixture until potatoes are golden brown and heated through. (May be made ahead and kept warm in a low oven.)

NOTE: Baked potatoes that will be further cooked in another recipe should be baked at 400° for 30–45 minutes. They are much easier to peel and dice when not fully cooked.

MENUS FOR HEARTY LUNCHES

★ Country Split Pea with Ham Soup ★

Corned Beef with Coleslaw on Rye

Fresh Fruit

★ Cream of Chicken Rice Soup ★

Smoked Salmon on a Bagel

Jam Bars (see page 52)

★ Oyster Stew ★

★ Monte Cristo ★

Shortbread (see page 103)

★ Beef Barley Soup ★

★ Curried Fruit Salad ★

French Bread

★ Brownies ★

★ Carrot Soup ★

Genoa Salami and Provolone Sandwich

Green Grapes with Sour Cream and Brown Sugar

★ Cream of Broccoli Soup ★

Ham and Cheese Croissant

★ Chocolate Macaroons ★

★ Beef Stew ★

French Bread

Date Bars

COUNTRY SPLIT PEA WITH HAM SOUP

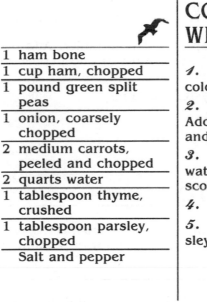

1	ham bone
1	cup ham, chopped
1	pound green split peas
1	onion, coarsely chopped
2	medium carrots, peeled and chopped
2	quarts water
1	tablespoon thyme, crushed
1	tablespoon parsley, chopped
	Salt and pepper

1. Place ham bone in a 4 quart stockpot; cover with cold water. Bring water to boil.

2. Rinse split peas, drain and add to boiling water. Add onions, ham, carrots, thyme, parsley, and salt and pepper to taste.

3. Boil moderately fast for 1½ hours. (Add more water if necessary.) Stir occasionally to prevent scorching.

4. Remove ham bone. Cool and refrigerate.

5. Reheat before serving. Sprinkle with fresh parsley.

CREAM OF CHICKEN RICE SOUP

4	cups chicken stock
¼	cup rice
1	carrot, peeled and diced
1	stalk celery, diced
1	small onion, diced
2	teaspoons thyme, crumbled
1	tablespoon parsley, chopped
1	cup cooked chicken meat, diced
1	cup heavy cream
	Salt and white pepper

1. Bring chicken stock to boiling. Add rice, carrot, celery, onion, and thyme. Simmer, covered, for 30 minutes.

2. Add chicken, cream, salt and white pepper to taste.

3. Reheat before serving.

OYSTER STEW

4 cups heavy cream
1 quart oysters, drained
Salt and pepper
4 teaspoons butter
Dash nutmeg

1. Heat cream in top of a double boiler. Add oysters, heat until edges curl. Add salt and pepper to taste, butter and nutmeg.

2. Serve hot with oyster crackers.

MONTE CRISTO

8 slices white bread
4 slices turkey
4 slices boiled ham
4 slices Swiss cheese
Dijon-style mustard
3 eggs
½ cup milk
Dash nutmeg
4 tablespoons butter

1. Spread 4 slices of bread with mustard. Layer meats and cheese over mustard. Top with remaining bread.

2. Beat eggs with milk and nutmeg.

3. Melt butter in large skillet. Dip sandwiches in egg mixture. Sauté until golden and cheese begins to melt. Turn. Brown remaining side.

NOTE: These sandwiches may be completely prepared, frozen, and reheated in the oven on medium heat for 20 minutes.

BEEF BARLEY SOUP

1 pound stew beef
1 soup bone
1 teaspoon salt
¼ teaspoon pepper
1 bay leaf
3 carrots, pared and sliced
¾ cup celery, chopped
½ cup onion, chopped
1 10-ounce can good beef bouillon
¼ cup dry red wine
1 teaspoon Worcestershire sauce
1 tablespoon basil, chopped
½ cup barley

1. Put beef and soup bone in a 3-quart Dutch oven; cover with cold water (about 3½ cups). Add salt, pepper and bay leaf. Bring to a boil. Add carrots, celery and onion; cover and simmer about 2–2½ hours or until meat is tender.

2. Discard bone and bay leaf. Add bouillon, wine, Worcestershire sauce, basil and barley. Cover and simmer 30–45 minutes or until barley is cooked.

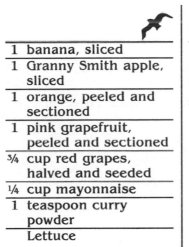

CURRIED FRUIT SALAD

1 banana, sliced
1 Granny Smith apple, sliced
1 orange, peeled and sectioned
1 pink grapefruit, peeled and sectioned
¾ cup red grapes, halved and seeded
¼ cup mayonnaise
1 teaspoon curry powder
Lettuce

1. Combine all ingredients thoroughly, but gently. Chill.

2. Serve on a bed of lettuce.

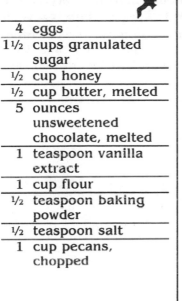

BROWNIES

4 eggs
1½ cups granulated sugar
½ cup honey
½ cup butter, melted
5 ounces unsweetened chocolate, melted
1 teaspoon vanilla extract
1 cup flour
½ teaspoon baking powder
½ teaspoon salt
1 cup pecans, chopped

Oven temperature: 350°

1. Beat together eggs, sugar, honey, butter and chocolate.

2. Add vanilla, flour, baking powder and salt, mixing after each addition.

3. Stir in nuts.

4. Pour into a greased and floured 9 x 13-inch pan. Bake in a preheated oven for 30 minutes.

5. Let cool 1 hour before cutting.

Yield: 24.

CARROT SOUP

3 cups chicken stock
1 small onion, chopped
4 carrots, peeled and
    sliced
⅛ teaspoon nutmeg
1 tablespoon
    Worcestershire sauce
1 clove garlic, minced
    Dash Tabasco

1. Simmer all ingredients until tender, about 15 minutes.

2. Remove half of carrots. Set aside. Puree mixture. Add reserved carrots.

3. Reheat before serving.

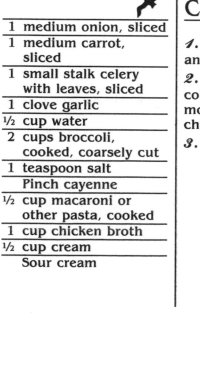

CREAM OF BROCCOLI SOUP

1 medium onion, sliced
1 medium carrot,
    sliced
1 small stalk celery
    with leaves, sliced
1 clove garlic
½ cup water
2 cups broccoli,
    cooked, coarsely cut
1 teaspoon salt
    Pinch cayenne
½ cup macaroni or
    other pasta, cooked
1 cup chicken broth
½ cup cream
    Sour cream

1. In a saucepan put onion, carrot, celery, garlic and water and simmer, covered, for 10 minutes. Cool.

2. Place mixture in blender container and add broccoli, salt, cayenne and macaroni. Cover and turn motor on high. Remove cover and, with motor on, add chicken broth and cream.

3. Serve hot with a dollop of sour cream.

CHOCOLATE MACAROONS

3 egg whites
6 ounces semisweet
   chocolate, melted
⅓ cup granulated sugar
1 teaspoon vanilla
   extract
4 ounces flaked
   coconut

Oven temperature: 375°

1. Beat egg whites until they form stiff peaks. Fold in remaining ingredients.

2. Drop cookies by teaspoonsful onto an ungreased baking sheet lined with waxed paper.

3. Bake in a preheated oven for 15–20 minutes.

BEEF STEW

1½ pounds stew beef
¾ cup peas (fresh or
   frozen)
¾ cup carrots, sliced
1½ cups onion,
   chopped
   Salt and pepper
1 cup beef broth
¼ cup red wine
1 potato, sliced
1 bay leaf
1½ tablespoons butter
1½ tablespoons flour

Oven temperature: 275°

1. Combine all ingredients in a covered casserole.

2. Bake in a preheated oven for 5 hours; or in a slow cooker for 7 hours.

3. Refrigerate or freeze.

4. Before serving reheat on stove top or in oven. Add 1½ tablespoons butter mixed with 1½ tablespoons flour to thicken, if desired. Simmer an additional 5 minutes.

MENUS FOR HEARTY SUPPERS

★ Grilled Ham Steaks ★
★ Bourbon Baked Beans ★
★ Cabbage and Pineapple Salad ★
★ Herb Bread (see page 97) ★
★ Apple Crisp ★

★ Tarragon Chicken Breasts ★
Rice
Green Beans with Toasted Almonds
★ Strawberry Tarts (see page 87) ★

★ Steak Diane ★
Baked Potatoes with Sour Cream and Caviar
Pea Pods with Tiny Peas
★ Blueberries with Lemon Cream (see page 115) ★

★ Lobster & Artichoke Casserole ★
Tossed Salad
Rolls
★ Chocolate Mousse (see page 103) ★

★ Chicken Florentine ★
Rice
★ Waldorf Salad ★
★ Chocolate Amaretto Cheesecake ★

★ Sea Scallop Sauté ★
Brown Rice
Broccoli with Lemon Butter
★ Almond Pound Cake with Raspberries (see page 123) ★

★ Capellini with White Clam Sauce ★
Green Salad
★ Garlic Bread (see page 32) ★
★ Strawberries Romanoff (see page 122) ★

GRILLED HAM STEAKS

2	large ham steaks
¼	cup pure maple syrup
1	tablespoon Dijon-style mustard

1. Combine maple syrup and mustard.

2. Brush ham steaks with syrup mixture.

3. Grill over hot coals about 7–8 minutes per side, basting occasionally.

BOURBON BAKED BEANS

3½	cups water
¾	pound dried navy or pea beans (about 1½ cups)
¼	pound bacon
1	medium onion, sliced
¼	cup brown sugar, packed
1	tablespoon molasses
1	teaspoon salt
¼	teaspoon dry mustard
⅛	teaspoon pepper
¼	cup bourbon

Oven temperature: 350°

1. Soak beans in 3½ cups of water overnight. Heat beans to boiling in the same water; cover and simmer until tender, 1–2 hours. Drain beans, reserving liquid.

2. Layer beans, onion and bacon in a 3-quart bean pot or casserole. Mix brown sugar, molasses, salt, mustard, pepper and bourbon with reserved bean liquid; pour over beans.

3. Cover and cook in a preheated oven for 3 hours. Uncover and cook until beans are of desired consistency, about 30 minutes. Cool. Refrigerate.

4. Before serving bring beans to room temperature and reheat in moderate oven for 30–40 minutes.

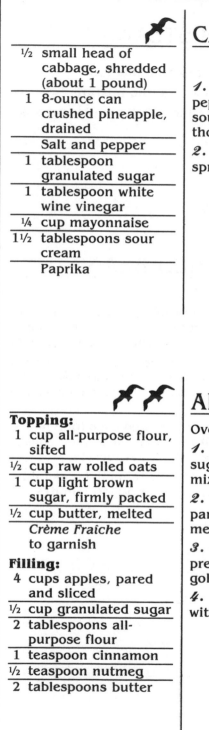

CABBAGE & PINEAPPLE SALAD

½ small head of cabbage, shredded (about 1 pound)

1 8-ounce can crushed pineapple, drained

Salt and pepper

1 tablespoon granulated sugar

1 tablespoon white wine vinegar

¼ cup mayonnaise

1½ tablespoons sour cream

Paprika

1. Combine cabbage and pineapple. Add salt and pepper to taste; add sugar, vinegar, mayonnaise, and sour cream. Mix together to combine ingredients thoroughly.

2. Before serving, place in an attractive bowl and sprinkle with paprika.

APPLE CRISP

Topping:

1 cup all-purpose flour, sifted

½ cup raw rolled oats

1 cup light brown sugar, firmly packed

½ cup butter, melted

Crème Fraîche to garnish

Filling:

4 cups apples, pared and sliced

½ cup granulated sugar

2 tablespoons all-purpose flour

1 teaspoon cinnamon

½ teaspoon nutmeg

2 tablespoons butter

Oven temperature: 375°

1. For topping: Combine flour, oats and brown sugar, mixing well. With a fork, stir in butter until mixture is crumbly.

2. For filling: In a lightly greased 8-inch square pan, combine apples, sugar, flour, cinnamon and nutmeg; stir to mix well. Dot with butter.

3. Sprinkle topping evenly over filling. Bake in a preheated oven 35–45 minutes or until topping is golden brown and apples are tender.

4. May be served warmed or at room temperature with *crème fraîche*, if desired.

TARRAGON CHICKEN BREASTS

2 whole chicken breasts, boned and halved

Salt and freshly ground pepper

2 tablespoons flour

¼ cup butter

2 tablespoons shallots, chopped

⅓ cup dry white Bordeaux wine

½ teaspoon dried tarragon

¾ cup chicken broth

⅓ cup heavy cream

1. Skin the chicken breasts. Sprinkle with salt and pepper and dredge with flour. Reserve remaining flour.

2. In a large skillet heat 3 tablespoons of butter; add chicken and brown on both sides. Transfer to a heated platter. Add shallots to the skillet and sauté briefly. Add wine.

3. Cook liquid over high heat until nearly evaporated, while scraping loose all the brown particles.

4. Add reserved flour and stir to make a paste. Sprinkle with tarragon and stir in chicken broth.

5. Return chicken to the skillet, cover and cook until tender, about 15–20 minutes. Transfer chicken to a heated platter and keep hot. Add remaining butter and cream to the skillet; heat, stirring, and pour sauce over the chicken. Serve immediately.

STEAK DIANE

2 fillet steaks

3 tablespoons butter

2 tablespoons Cognac, heated

4 tablespoons sherry

2 tablespoons sweet butter, creamed with 2 teaspoons chopped chives

1. Butterfly steaks and pound thin with a mallet.

2. Heat 3 tablespoons butter in a skillet. Add the steaks and cook quickly, turning once, about 1–2 minutes per side.

3. Add Cognac and flame. Add sherry and sweet butter creamed with chives. Serve steaks on a heated platter with the sauce. Serves 2.

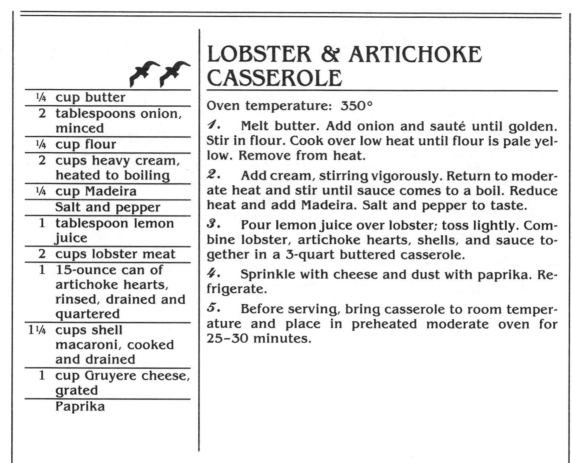

LOBSTER & ARTICHOKE CASSEROLE

¼ cup butter

2 tablespoons onion, minced

¼ cup flour

2 cups heavy cream, heated to boiling

¼ cup Madeira

Salt and pepper

1 tablespoon lemon juice

2 cups lobster meat

1 15-ounce can of artichoke hearts, rinsed, drained and quartered

1¼ cups shell macaroni, cooked and drained

1 cup Gruyere cheese, grated

Paprika

Oven temperature: 350°

1. Melt butter. Add onion and sauté until golden. Stir in flour. Cook over low heat until flour is pale yellow. Remove from heat.

2. Add cream, stirring vigorously. Return to moderate heat and stir until sauce comes to a boil. Reduce heat and add Madeira. Salt and pepper to taste.

3. Pour lemon juice over lobster; toss lightly. Combine lobster, artichoke hearts, shells, and sauce together in a 3-quart buttered casserole.

4. Sprinkle with cheese and dust with paprika. Refrigerate.

5. Before serving, bring casserole to room temperature and place in preheated moderate oven for 25–30 minutes.

WALDORF SALAD

3 apples, pared and sliced

2 stalks celery

½ cup walnuts, chopped

½ cup raisins

⅓ cup mayonnaise (see recipe)

Nutmeg

1. Combine apples, celery, walnuts and raisins. Add mayonnaise and mix well. Chill.

2. Sprinkle with nutmeg before serving.

CHICKEN FLORENTINE

1	pound spinach
4	tablespoons butter
1	clove garlic, mashed
	Dash basil
	Dash marjoram
4	tablespoons flour
1¼	cups heavy cream
	Meat from one 3½ pound cooked chicken
¾	cup chicken broth
¾	cup Parmesan cheese, grated
	Salt and pepper

Oven temperature: 400°

1. Cook spinach. Drain and chop.

2. Melt 1 tablespoon butter. Add garlic, basil and marjoram. Add flour and mix well. Add ½ cup heavy cream and spinach. Place spinach mixture in the bottom of a shallow casserole.

3. Cover with chicken meat.

4. Melt 3 tablespoons butter; add 3 tablespoons flour. Add ¾ cup cream, chicken broth and salt and pepper to taste. Cook stirring constantly until thickened. Pour over chicken.

5. Sprinkle with Parmesan cheese. Refrigerate or freeze.

6. To serve, bake in a preheated oven for 20 minutes or until cheese is bubbling.

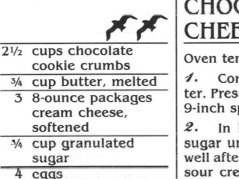

CHOCOLATE AMARETTO CHEESECAKE

2½	cups chocolate cookie crumbs
¾	cup butter, melted
3	8-ounce packages cream cheese, softened
¾	cup granulated sugar
4	eggs
6	ounces semisweet chocolate, melted and cooled
2	cups sour cream
½	cup plus 2 tablespoons Amaretto liqueur
1	teaspoon vanilla extract
	Sliced almonds, toasted

Oven temperature: 350°

1. Combine cookie crumbs with ½ cup melted butter. Press firmly in bottom and 2 inches up sides of a 9-inch springform pan. Chill.

2. In large mixing bowl, beat cream cheese and sugar until fluffy. Add eggs, one at a time, beating well after each addition. Blend in chocolate and 1 cup sour cream, ½ cup Amaretto, 4 tablespoons butter and vanilla. Pour into prepared crust.

3. Bake in a preheated oven 65 minutes or until just set.

4. Stir together remaining sour cream and Amaretto; spread over cheesecake. Return to oven for 3 minutes. Cool.

5. Cover and refrigerate. Garnish with almonds.

Yield: 12 servings.

NOTE: I usually wrap slices individually in waxed paper and transport in a covered plastic container.

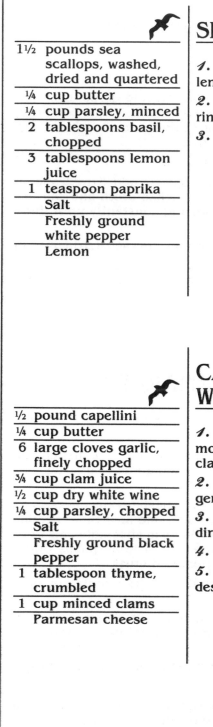

SEA SCALLOP SAUTÉ

1½ pounds sea scallops, washed, dried and quartered
¼ cup butter
¼ cup parsley, minced
2 tablespoons basil, chopped
3 tablespoons lemon juice
1 teaspoon paprika
Salt
Freshly ground white pepper
Lemon

1. In a large skillet, melt butter. Add parsley, basil, lemon juice, paprika, salt and pepper to taste.

2. Add scallops. Cook quickly over high heat, stirring occasionally until golden brown, 5–10 minutes.

3. Garnish with fresh lemon.

CAPELLINI WITH WHITE CLAM SAUCE

½ pound capellini
¼ cup butter
6 large cloves garlic, finely chopped
¾ cup clam juice
½ cup dry white wine
¼ cup parsley, chopped
Salt
Freshly ground black pepper
1 tablespoon thyme, crumbled
1 cup minced clams
Parmesan cheese

1. Heat butter; add garlic and cook 1 minute over moderate heat. Stir in flour with a wire whisk. Add clam juice and wine. Continue stirring.

2. Add parsley, salt, pepper and thyme. Simmer gently for 10 minutes.

3. Meanwhile cook capellini according to package directions.

4. Add clams and heat through.

5. Serve over capellini with Parmesan cheese, if desired.

INDEX

Danish, cheese, 73
Danish sandwiches, 42
Date pinwheels, 48
Day sail, 25–56
  menus, 26–28
Dessert(s)
  almond macaroons, 77
  almond pound cake, 123
  almond spritz cookies, 128
  almond-filled brownies, 43
  apple crisp, 148
  apple walnut cake, 31
  apricot pound cake, 46
  banana sauté with Grand
    Marnier, 97
  bananas poached in white
    wine with chocolate-orange
    sauce, 91
  blueberries in lemon cream,
    115
  blueberry crisp, 33
  blueberry turnovers, 79
  brownies, 143
  carrot cake, 67
  chocolate Amaretto
    cheesecake, 151
  chocolate cake with
    raspberries & chocolate
    sauce, 62
  chocolate chestnut brownies,
    129
  chocolate chip brownies, 50
  chocolate chip pound cake, 56
  chocolate chunk cookies, 101
  chocolate macaroons, 145
  chocolate mint icebox cake,
    78
  chocolate mousse, 103
  chocolate walnut upside down
    cake, 72
  chocolate, white chocolate
    chunk cookies, 34
  chocolate-cheese brownies,
    121
  chocolate-orange truffles, 112
  coconut delights, 124
  coconut macaroon cupcakes,
    37
  date pinwheels, 48
  fruit compote, fresh, 68
  jam bars, 52
  lemon squares, 44
  milk chocolate fudge, 42
  mincemeat cookies, 55
  mixed fruit bars, 40
  oatmeal raisin cookies,
    special, 70
  orange compote, 83
  plum clafouti, 81
  raspberry cheesecake, 118
  raspberry kuchen, 82
  raspberry roulade, 76
  raspberry thumbprints, 89
  shortbread, 103
  strawberries Romanoff, 122
  strawberry tarts, 87
Deviled eggs, 100
Dill
  mayonnaise, 53
  sauce, smoked pheasant with,
    45
Dressing. See Salad dressing
Drinks. See also Beverages
  Bloody Mary, 115
  tomato juice, fresh, 87
  mimosas, 104
Duck breast, smoked, salad, 35

Egg(s)
  Adrienne, 115
  Benedict, 104
  Benedict Arnold, 92
  curried, 107
  deviled, 100
  magnifique, 60
  mariners', 79
  omelet
    bacon & cheese, 72
    ham, with cheese sauce, 111
    Mexican, 98
    walnut & cheese, 83
    western, 131
  scramble, hearty ham &, 135
  scrambled, en croute, 88
  scrambled, with smoked
    salmon, 119
  twist bread, 108
Elegant weekend, 93–124
  menus, 95, 106, 116
Endive & grapefruit salad, 61
English muffin bread, 135
Entrées. See also Sandwich(es)
  beef stew, 145
  boursin chicken breasts, 86
  broccoli & ham quiche, 63
  Cajun swordfish grill, 90
  capellini with white clam
    sauce, 152
  chicken Florentine, 151
  chicken stir fry, 83
  chicken with almonds, 110
  chilled roast tenderloin of
    beef, 121
  cold poached salmon with
    sauce Remoulade, 113
  coq au vin, 133
  corned beef hash, 131

Cornish game hens with
    raspberry glaze, 102
  faux piccata Milanese, 75
  flank steak in red wine
    marinade, 65
  grilled ham steaks, 147
  grilled lamb chops with
    rosemary mint sauce, 96
  grilled pork tenderloin in wine
    marinade, 61
  lasagne, 128
  lobster artichoke casserole,
    150
  lobster Parisienne, 117
  medallions of beef with
    Madeira sauce, 81
  oven fried chicken, 71
  oyster stew, 142
  pan fried steak, 139
  pasta primavera, 71
  scallop kabobs, 107
  sea scallop sauté, 152
  shrimp, cauliflower & snow
    peas in crème fraîche, 33
  shrimp with tomatoes and feta
    cheese, 59
  smoked trout with horseradish
    sauce, 123
  steak Diane, 149
  tarragon chicken breasts, 149
  tomato and basil quiche, 124

Faux piccata Milanese, 75
Feta cheese
  artichoke hearts with, 35
  shrimp with tomatoes and, 59
Fish. See also Seafood
  salmon, cold poached, with
    sauce Remoulade, 113
  salmon, smoked, scrambled
    eggs with, 119
  salmon steaks, grilled lime, 77
  swordfish grill, Cajun, 90
  trout, smoked, with
    horseradish sauce, 123
Flank steak in red wine
    marinade, 65
Florentine rice, 78
Food processor mayonnaise, 53
French bread, 100
French rolls, sourdough, 60
French toast, 127
Fresh fruit compote, 68
Fresh tomato juice, 87
Fried chicken, oven, 71
Frizzled ham, 139
Frosting, cream cheese, 67

T

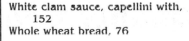

Other Quality Cookbooks

SIMPLY ELEGANT COUNTRY FOODS: Downhome Goes Uptown
by Carol Lowe-Clay

An outrageously good cook brings country cooking to its pinnacle. A cookbook that's not fussy, not trendy—simply elegant. Everything from country fresh *Pizza Rustica* to *Crumbed Chicken in Wine Sauce, Country Pork Supper, Sweet Cream Scones with Honey Butter* to *Whipped Cream Cake with Almond Custard Filling.* Over 100 recipes capturing the freshness of the moment!

160 pages, 8 x 10, beautifully illustrated.
Quality paperback, $9.95

GOLDE'S HOMEMADE COOKIES
by Golde Hoffman Soloway

"Cookies are her chosen realm and how sweet a world it is to visit."
Publishers Weekly

Over 100 treasured recipes that defy description. Suffice it to say that no one could walk away from Golde's cookies without asking for another . . . plus the recipe.

144 pages, 8¼ x 7¼, illustrations.
Quality paperback, $8.95.

SUMMER IN A JAR: Making Pickles, Jams & More
by Andrea Chesman

"With recipes this simple and varied, it's hard to find an excuse not to preserve summer in one's cupboard."   Publishers Weekly

Chesman introduces single jar recipes so you can make pickles and relishes a single quart at a time. Plenty of low-sugar jams, marmalades, relishes. Pickles by the crock, too. Outstanding recipes.

160 pages, 8¼ x 7¼, illustrations.
Quality paperback, $8.95.

THE BROWN BAG COOKBOOK:
Nutritious Portable Lunches for Kids and Grown-Ups
by Sara Sloan

Here are more than 1,000 brown bag lunch ideas with 150 recipes for simple, quick, nutritious lunches.

192 pages, 8¼ x 7¼, illustrations.
Quality paperback, $8.95.

To order:

At your bookstore or order directly from Williamson Publishing. Send check, money order or charge on Visa or Mastercard to **Williamson Publishing Co., Church Hill Road, P.O. Box 185, Charlotte, Vermont 05445**. (Phone orders: 1-800-234-8791) Please add $2.50 for postage and handling. Satisfaction guaranteed or full refund without question or quibble.